孟子语录

金沛霖 李亚斯 编译

金沛霖 主编

中国华侨出版社

图书在版编目(CIP)数据

孟子语录:汉英对照 / 金沛霖主编. —北京:中国华侨出版社,2010.12
ISBN 978-7-5113-1001-9

Ⅰ.孟... Ⅱ.金... Ⅲ.孟轲(前 390~ 前 305)—语录—汉、英 Ⅳ.B222.5

中国版本图书馆 CIP 数据核字(2010)第 244518 号

● **孟子语录:汉英对照**

主　　编 / 金沛霖

责任编辑 / 崔卓力

装帧设计 / 袁剑锋

责任校对 / 吕　宏

经　　销 / 全国新华书店

开　　本 / 787×1092 毫米　1/16　印张 /16.5　字数 /216 千字

印　　刷 / 廊坊市华北石油华星印务有限公司

版　　次 / 2011 年 3 月第 1 版　2011 年 3 月第 1 次印刷

书　　号 / ISBN 978-7-5113-1001-9

定　　价 / 29.80 元

中国华侨出版社　北京市安定路 20 号院 3 号楼　邮编:100029
法律顾问:陈鹰律师事务所

编辑部:　(010) 64443056　64443979

发行部:　(010) 64443051　传真:(010) 64439708

网　　址:www.oveaschin.com

e-mail : oveaschin@sina.com

孟　子（约公元前 372—公元前 289）

Mencius (372 BCE—289 BCE)

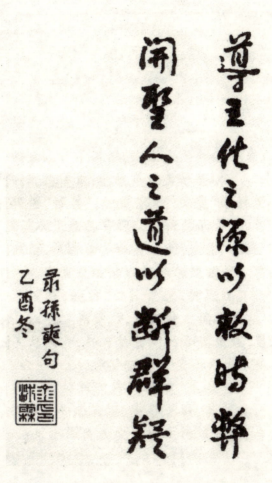

導王化之源以救時弊
開聖人之道以斷群疑

录孫奭句
乙酉冬

Proposing benevolent government, and practicing virtues, Mencius, together with Confucius, laid the foundation of Confucianism.

前　言

　　孔子创立的儒家学派，经由孟子继承与发展，终于成就一套完整的思想体系，也就是孔孟之道。

　　孟子提倡"性善"，把儒家的"仁爱"之说置于人的本性之中，强调人生来具有的人格价值和尊严；把"仁道"思想推广到政治、经济诸多社会方面，主张"王道"，反对"霸道"，指出人心向背是政治成败的决定因素。在此基础上孟子进一步发挥，提出"仁民爱物"的思想。认为不但人与人之间应以"仁"相待，人与万物之间也应以"仁"相待，从而达到人与人、人与万物之间的和谐发展，首次具体阐明了"天人合一"这一重要观念。孟子力主人们应在逆境中磨炼自己，养"浩然之气"，要有"乐以天下，忧以天下"的胸怀和"如欲平治天下，当今之世，舍我其谁"的志气。这些都已成为中华民族宝贵的文化遗产，至今仍有重大影响。

　　学习儒家思想，《孟子》一书不可不读。

编　者

A Note on the Quotations

Mencius was the most important Confucian philosopher after Confucius; the medieval to modern version of Confucianism has been dominated by his doctrines. His influence on Chinese philosophy and the Chinese point of view has been immense. The Mencius, the book that bears his name, is the most important work that recorded his ideas.

Mencius lived in the fourth century B. C. , during the Warring States period, an era of persistent political and social upheavals. He wished a moral and ordered life. Mencius believed the human nature is inherently good. The essence of this goodness was the compassion towards others. The reason for people' s not practicing good was due to they neglected this innate goodness. He advocated the actualization of the potential goodness of human nature through self—cultivation and moral education as the way to solve the political and social problems.

Mencius argued that people should be treated as moral beings. According to him the people are the most important element in a nation while the ruler is of the least importance. The ruler and government exist for the well—being of the people. Moreover, the general mood of morality in a society depends on the degree of material security. Hence, if a ruler can't provide this for his people then the people no longer have to be loyal.

Mencius often told coherent short tales with a moral. Sometimes he used analogical arguments, which were logically invalid, to defend his point of view. In a world of dialectic he said he had no alternative.

The quotations are selected from The Mencius to cover the main ideas of his doctrines. They are arranged by subjects to be easy to look up. There are ancient Chinese words which have different meanings in different contexts. For example, the word "xin" can have the meaning of "to believe", "indeed", or "being earnest in practicing virtues". Some important terms and concepts are listed in the appendix.

目　录
Contents

前 言

A Note on the Quotations ……………………… （ 1 ）

一、性 善

I. On Innate Goodness ……………………… （ 1 ）

二、教 育

II. On Education ……………………… （ 15 ）

三、修 身

III. On Self－cultivation ……………………… （ 33 ）

四、仁义、忠信

IV. On Benevolence, Uprightness, Faithfulness,
and Sincerity ……………………… （107）

五、王道、仁政

V. On Benevolent Government ……………………… （129）

六、君子与小人

VI. The Perfect Gentlemen vs. the Vulgar …………… （219）

七、富贵与贫贱

VII. On Riches and Honor, Poverty and Humbleness

……………………… （229）

八、生死与天命

VIII. On Life, Death, and the Appointment of Heaven

……………………… （237）

附录：重要的词汇和概念

Appendix: Important Terms and Concepts …………… （242）

The Quotations by Mencius

性善

On Innate Goodness

一

人皆有不忍人之心。先王有不忍人之心，斯有不忍人之政矣。以不忍人之心，行不忍人之政，治天下可运之掌上。

所以谓人皆有不忍人之心者，今人乍见孺子将入于井，皆有怵惕恻隐之心。非所以内交于孺子之父母也，非所以要誉于乡党朋友也，非恶其声而然也。

由是观之，无恻隐之心，非人也；无羞恶之心，非人也；无辞让之心，非人也；无是非之心，非人也。恻隐之心，仁之端也；羞恶之心，义之端也；辞让之心，礼之端也；是非之心，智之端也。人之有是四端也，犹其有四体也。有是四端而自谓不能者，自贼者也；谓其君不能者，贼其君者也。

（《孟子》公孙丑章句上）

【译文】

任何正常人都有同情怜悯他人伤痛的心。古代的帝王有这样的同情怜悯的心，所以就有同情怜恤他人的政策。用同情怜悯他人的心，实施同情怜恤他人的政策，治理天下就会像在手掌心里面运转小物件一样容易。

之所以说每个人都有同情怜悯他人伤痛的心，是因为如果人突然看见小孩子要掉进井里，会立即觉察到要发生的不幸而感到惊恐。这并不是因为想要结交这孩子的父母，不是因为想在乡邻朋友中博得赞誉，也不是因为不喜欢冷漠的恶名才产生这种心情的。

由此看来，没有同情怜悯的心，不是真正的人。没有耻己之不善和憎人之不善的心，不是真正的人；没有谦让的心，不是真正的人；没有辨别是非的心，不是真正的人。同情怜悯的心，是本心中的仁的萌芽；耻己之不善和憎人之不善的心，是本心中的义的萌芽；谦让的心，是本心中的礼的萌芽；辨别是非的心，是本心中的智的萌芽。人有这四种萌芽，就像有四肢一样自然。人有这四种萌芽却认为自己无法发展它们，是害自己的人。认为他的君王无法发展它们，是害君王的人。

All men have a heart – mind that is sensitive to the sufferings of others. The ancient Kings had this sympathetic heart – mind, and thus adopted benevolent policies. If benevolent policies were put into practice with a sympathetic heart – mind, to rule the land under Heaven will be as easy as to make a small thing go round in the palm.

The reason why I say that all men have a heart – mind that is sensitive to the sufferings of others is this: if men suddenly see a child about to fall into a well, they will have a feeling of alarm and danger. They will feel so, not because they seek to get in good with the child's parents, not because they want a good reputation among their neighbors and friends, and not because they dislike the reputation of having been unmoved by such a thing.

From this manifestation we can see that if one is without the feeling of sympathy, one is not a human. If one is without the capacity to feel shame for not being benevolent by himself, and detestation for not being benevolent by others, one is not a human. If one is without the feeling of modesty, one is not a human. If one is without the feeling of true and false, one is not a human.

The feeling of sympathy is the sprout of benevolence in the original heart – mind. The feeling of shame and detestation is the sprout of uprightness in the original heart – mind. The feeling of modesty is the sprout of etiquette in the original heart – mind. The feeling of true and false is the sprout of wisdom in the original heart – mind.

Men have these four sprouts just as natural as they have their four limbs. Having these four sprouts but to think of oneself that one is unable to develop them is to do harm to oneself. To think that one's sovereign is unable to develop them is to do harm to one's sovereign.

大人者，不失其赤子之心者也。

（《孟子》离娄章句下）

【译文】

杰出的人是那些内心像新生的婴儿一样纯真的人。

The great man is he who still retains the innocent heart of a child.

天下之言性也，则故而已矣。故者以利为本。所恶于智者，为其凿也。如智者若禹之行水也，则无恶于智矣。禹之行水也，行其所无事也。如智者亦行其所无事，则智亦大矣。天之高也，星辰之远也，苟求其故，千岁之日至，可坐而致也。

（《孟子》离娄章句下）

【译文】

人们谈论人和事物的本性，都是看表面的现象。这些表面现象必然遵循着本性。人们厌恶乱用智慧，是因为有人牵强地解释现象。要是人使用智慧时像禹治水那样顺其自然，人们就不会厌恶智慧了。天虽然高，星辰虽然远，但如果从现象探求本质，就是一千年以后的冬至，也可以坐着推算出来。

When people speak about the nature of things, they only look at the surface of things. The outward appearance must follow the essence. The reason why people dislike wise men is because they give strained interpretations of phenomena. If these wise men would just apply wisdom in accordance with its natural tendency like Yu did when he regulated rivers and watercourses, then there would not be such a dislike of wise men. There is heaven so high; there are the stars so distant. But if we can see through the appearance to the essence, we may, while sitting in our places, calculate the time when the Winter Solstice will be a thousand years later.

告子曰："性，犹杞柳也；义，犹杯棬也。以人性为仁义，犹以杞柳为杯棬。"

孟子曰："子能顺杞柳之性而以为杯棬乎？将戕贼杞柳而后以为杯棬也？如将戕贼杞柳而以为杯棬，则亦将戕贼人以为仁义与？率天下之人而祸仁义者，必子之言夫！"

（《孟子》告子章句上）

【译文】

告子说："天生的资质就像是杞柳树；义就像是把木料弯曲做成的杯子。让人性归于仁义，就像是把杞柳树弯曲做成杯子一样。"

孟子说："你是顺着杞柳树的天生资质来制作杯子呢？还是破坏了杞柳树的天生资质来制作杯子呢？要是破坏杞柳树的天生资质来制作杯子，那也要破坏人的天生资质来使人有仁义吗？让天下人以为仁义会破坏天生资质的，一定是你的这种观点！"

The philosopher Gao said, "The inborn constitution of human being is like a willow tree; and uprightness is like the cups and bowls that are carved out of the wood. To make human nature to be benevolent and upright is like carving cups and bowls out of the willow wood."

Mencius said, "Can you make cups and bowls following the nature of the willow? It is by doing injury to the willow that you make cups and bowls. If we do injury to the willow to make cups and bowls, should we also do injury to human being to make them benevolent and upright? Your words would certainly lead people on to believe benevolence and uprightness will do injury to their inborn constitution."

告子曰："性犹湍水也，决诸东方则东流，决诸西方则西流。人性之无分于善不善也，犹水之无分于东西也。"

孟子曰："水信无分于东西。无分于上下乎？人性之善也，犹水之就下也。人无有不善，水无有不下。今夫水，搏而跃之，可使过颡；激而行之，可使在山。是岂水之性哉？其势则然也。人之可使为不善，其性亦犹是也。"

（《孟子》告子章句上）

【译文】

告子说："天生的资质就像湍急的水，东边出现缺口就向东流，西边出现缺口就向西流。人的天生资质无所谓善和不善，就像水无所谓向东流和向西流一样。"

孟子说："水的确无所谓向东流和向西流，但是，也无所谓向上流和向下流吗？人本性向善，就像水往低处流一样。人的本性没有不善良的，水没有不向低处流的。当然，如果拍打水能让它飞溅起来，可以高过额头；加压迫使它倒行，能使它流上山岗。这难道是水的本性吗？是形势迫使它如此的。可以迫使人做坏事，但人的本性还是不变。"

The philosopher Gao said, "Man's inborn constitution is like whirling water. Make an outlet for it to the east, and it will flow to the east; make an outlet for it to the west, and it will flow to the west. Man's nature is indifferent to good and evil, just as the water is indifferent to the east and west."

Mencius replied, "Water indeed is indifferent to the east or west, but does it flow indifferently upwards and downwards? The tendency of man's original nature to benevolence is like the tendency of water to flow downwards. There is no man who does not have this inborn tendency to benevolence. There is no water that does not flow downwards. Of course, by striking water and making it splash, you can cause it to fly over your forehead; and, by pressing it, you may force it flow upwards and up a hill. Could it be said that this is the nature of water? It is that way because of the circumstances. Man can be caused to do what is not benevolent, but their original nature remains invariant."

乃若其情，则可以为善矣，乃所谓善也。若夫为不善，非才之罪也。恻隐之心，人皆有之；羞恶之心，人皆有之；恭敬之心，人皆有之；是非之心，人皆有之。恻隐之心，仁也；羞恶之心，义也；恭敬之心，礼也；是非之心，智也。仁义礼智，非由外铄我也，我固有之也，弗思而矣。故曰："求则得之，舍则失之。"或相倍蓰而无算者，不能尽其才者也。诗曰："天生蒸民，有物有则。民之秉夷，好是懿德。"孔子曰："为此诗者，其知道乎！故有物必有则，民之秉夷也，故好是懿德。"

（《孟子》告子章句上）

【译文】

　　从人的天生资质看，都可以使他们善良，这就是我说人性本善的意思。至于说有些人不善良，不能归罪于天生的资质。同情怜悯的心，人人都有；耻己之不善和憎人之不善的心，人人都有；谦让的心，人人都有；辨别是非的心，人人都有。同情怜悯的心是仁的产物；耻己之不善和憎人之不善的心是义的产物；谦让的心是礼的产物；辨别是非的心是智的产物。仁、义、礼、智都不是由外在的因素给予我的，而是我本身固有的，只不过平时没有去想它们因而不觉得罢了。所以说："把握住就能留存，放弃就会失去。"人与人之间有相差一倍、五倍甚至无数倍的，正是由于没有充分发挥他们的天生资质的缘故。《诗经》上说："上天孕育了人类，有事物就一定有法则。百姓掌握了这些法则，就会有美好的品德。"孔子说："写这首诗的人真懂得道啊！有事物就一定有法则；百姓掌握了这些法则，就会有美好的品德。"

On the basis of people's natural endowments, they can become benevolent. This is what I mean in saying that the human nature is good. As for their becoming not benevolent, the blame can't be put on their natural endowments. All men have the feeling of sympathy in their original heart – mind. All men have the capacity to feel shame for not being benevolent by himself, and detestation for not being benevolent by others. All men have the feeling of modesty. All men have the capacity to distinguish trueness and falseness. The feeling of sympathy is the outcome of benevolence in the heart – mind. The feeling of shame and detestation is the outcome of uprightness in the heart - mind. The feeling of modesty is the outcome of etiquette in the heart - mind. The feeling of trueness and falseness is the outcome of wisdom in the heart - mind. Benevolence, uprightness, etiquette and wisdom are not infused into us from without. We inherently have them. Only we do not reflect on them. Hence, it is said, "Hold it fast, and it remains with you. Abandon it, and you lose it." Men differ from one another by two, five or countless times. This difference is because some are unable to fully develop their natural endowments. It is said in the Book of Poetry,

"Heaven creates mankind,

If there is a thing, there is its principle.

And if the people hold the principle fast,

They will have beautiful virtue."

Confucius said, "The writer of this poem understood indeed the principle of our nature! If there is a thing, there must be its principle. And if the people hold the principle of their nature fast, they will consequently have beautiful virtue."

富岁，子弟多赖；凶岁，子弟多暴，非天之降才尔殊也，其所以陷溺其心者然也。

（《孟子》告子章句上）

【译文】

丰收年，年轻人大多随和；灾荒年，年轻人大多横暴。不是天生的资质如此不同，是由于外部环境使他们的心有所改变。

In years of good harvest the children of the people are mostly amiable, while in years of bad harvest the most of them are perverse and violent. This is not because Heaven confers down so different endowments on them, but because the circumstances can change their minds.

牛山之木尝美矣，以其郊于大国也，斧斤伐之，可以为美乎？是其日夜之所息，雨露之所润，非无萌蘖之生焉，牛羊又从而牧之，是以若彼濯濯也。人见其濯濯也，以为未尝有材焉，此岂山之性也哉？

虽存乎人者，岂无仁义之心哉？其所以放其良心者，亦犹斧斤之于木也，旦旦而伐之，可以为美乎？其日夜之所息，平旦之气，其好恶与人相近也者几希，则其旦昼之所为，有梏亡之矣。梏之反复，则其夜气不足以存；夜气不足以存，则其违禽兽不远矣。人见其禽兽也，而以为未尝有才焉者，是岂人之情也哉？

故苟得其养，无物不长；苟失其养，无物不消。孔子曰："操则存，舍则亡；出入无时，莫知其乡。"惟心之谓与？

（《孟子》告子章句上）

【译文】

牛山的树木曾经是很茂盛的，但是由于它在国都的郊外，经常被人们用斧子砍伐，怎么还能保持茂盛呢？树木日日夜夜都在生长，雨水露珠也滋润着它们，不是没长出新枝侧芽来，可是又有人赶着牛羊在那里放牧，所以就像这样光秃秃的了。人们看见牛山光秃秃的，以为它从来也没长过大树，这难道是山的本性吗？

在一些人身上也是如此，难道没有仁义之心吗？他们放任天生的善良之心失去，也像用斧头砍伐树木一样，天天砍伐，还可以保持茂盛吗？善良之心在夜深人静和没有外界打扰的时候，一定有所生长。这些在他心里激发出来的好恶和一般人相近的也有一点点。可是他白天的所作所为，又把它们窒息消亡了。反复窒息的结果，使他们夜里的休息不足以保存本心。夜里的休息不足以保存本心，也就和禽兽差不多了。人们见到这些人的所作所为和禽兽差不多，以为他们从来就没有过好的本心。这难道是人的本性如此吗？

所以只要得到滋养，没有什么东西不生长；只要失去滋养，没有什么东西不消亡。孔子过："把握住就能留存，放弃就会失去；显现的内容没有规律，也不知道它在哪里。"这说的就是人心吧？

The trees of the mount Niu were once luxuriant. But since the mountain was on the outskirts of the capital, the trees were hewn down with axes. How could it retain its luxuriance? The trees grew day and night, nourished by the rain and dew, they were not without new branches and lateral buds springing forth, but then came the cattle and sheep and browsed upon them. So the mountain is now barren. And when people see this barrenness, they think it was never finely wooded. But is this the nature of the mountain?

In the case of man, how could they lack the mind of benevolence and uprightness? The way in which a man loses his benevolence and uprightness of mind is like the way in which the trees are denuded by axes. Being chopped down day after day, how can it manifest its natural luxuriance? The benevolent mind surely grows in the still of night and when there is no external disturbance. To some extent, the likes and dislikes, which are proper to humanity, are aroused in the mind. But these feelings are suffocated and destroyed by what they do during the day. This suffocating taking place again and again, the revitalization in the night is not sufficient to preserve the original mind. Then the revitalization in the night is not sufficient to preserve the original mind, and the nature will become about the same with that of the beasts. When people see what they do are about the same with that of the beasts, they think that those creatures never had good original mind. How could this be man's original nature?

Therefore, if it is properly nourished, there is nothing that will not grow. If it loses its proper nourishment, there is nothing that will not die out. Confucius said, "Hold it fast, and it remains with you. Abandon it, and you lose it. Its manifestation has no regular pattern. No one knows its location." What

一

性

善 On Innate Goodness

else could he be talking about but the mind?

人之所不学而能者，其良能也；所不虑而知者，其良知也。孩提之童无不知爱其亲者，及其长也，无不知敬其兄也。亲亲，仁也；敬长，义也；无他，达之天下也。

（《孟子》尽心章句上）

【译文】

人不经学习就能做的，那是良能；不经思考就能知道的，那是良知。年幼的孩子，没有不知道要爱他们父母的；长大后，没有不知道要敬重他们兄长的。爱父母就是仁，敬兄长就是义，这没有别的原因，只因为仁和义是通行于天下的。

The ability possessed by men without having been acquired by learning is intuitive ability, and the knowledge possessed by them without the exercise of thought is their intuitive knowledge. Young children all know to love their parents, and when they are grown a little, they all know to love their elder brothers. Filial benevolence is the working of benevolence. Fraternal affection is the working of righteousness. There is no other reason for those feelings; they belong to all people under Heaven.

孟子语录

The Quotations by Mencius

教育

On Education

设为庠序学校以教之：庠者，养也；校者，教也；序者，射也。夏曰校，殷曰序，周曰庠，学则三代共之，皆所以明人伦也。人伦明于上，小民亲于下。

（《孟子》滕文公章句上）

【译文】

要办学校来教育百姓。"庠"是教养的意思；"校"是教育的意思；"序"是习射的意思。夏代叫"校"，商代叫"序"，周朝叫"庠"，至于大学，三代都叫"学"，都是阐明人和人之间的必然关系的。处于上层的人明白了人和人之间的必然关系，百姓间就会亲密。

A ruler should set up schools to educate the people, for example, 'Xiang', 'Xu', 'Xue', and 'Xiao'. 'Xiang' means 'breeding'. 'Xiao' means 'education'. 'Xu' means 'archery'. In Xia dynasty the name 'Xiao' was used; in Shang dynasty, that of 'Xu'; and by the Zhou dynasty, that of 'Xiang'. As to the 'Xue', they belonged to the three dynasties, and by that name. The object of them all is to clarify the inexorable relations between individuals. When the upper classes of society understand the inexorable relations between individuals, kindly feeling will prevail among the people.

中也养不中，才也养不才，故人乐有贤父兄也。如中也弃不中，才也弃不才，则贤不肖之相去，其闲不能以寸。

（《孟子》离娄章句下）

【译文】

　　道德修养好的人教育熏陶道德修养差的人，有才能和作为的人教育熏陶缺乏才能和作为的人。所以人人都乐于有道德修养好并且有才能和作为的父亲和兄长。如果道德修养好的人抛弃道德修养差的人，有才能和作为的人抛弃缺乏才能和作为的人，那么，所谓好与不好之间的差别，也就相近得不能用寸来区分了。

Those who possess virtue nurture those who do not, and those who have talents nurture those who have not. Hence, men rejoice in having fathers and elder brothers who possess virtue and talents. If they who possess virtue abandon those who do not, and they who have talents abandon those who have not, then the space between the gifted and the ungifted will not admit an inch.

博学而详说之，将以反说约也。

（《孟子》离娄章句下）

【译文】

广博地学习，详尽地讨论，是为了能简约地去说明大意。

In studying comprehensively and discussing thoroughly what is learned, one may be able to go back and set forth in brief what is essential.

以善服人者，未有能服人者也；以善养人，然后能服天下。天下不心服而王者，未之有也。

（《孟子》离娄章句下）

【译文】

单凭善就想让别人归服，是不能够使人归服的；教育人使人也变善，才能让天下的人归服。天下的人心不归服而想让天下归服，这是没有过的事。

Never has he who would by being benevolent make people yield been able to make them yield. If one can nourish people so that they will become benevolent, then he will be able to make people under Heaven yield. It is impossible that anyone should make people under Heaven yield if their hearts have not yielded.

孟子曰："无或乎王之不智也，虽有天下易生之物也，一日暴之，十日寒之。未有能生者也。吾见亦罕矣，吾退而寒之者至矣。吾如有萌焉何哉！今夫弈之为数，小数也；不专心致志，则不得也。弈秋，通国之善弈者也。使弈秋诲二人弈，其一人专心致志，惟弈秋之为听。一人虽听之，一心以为有鸿鹄将至，思援弓缴而射之，虽与之俱学，弗若之矣。为是其智弗若与？曰：非然也。"

(《孟子》告子章句上)

【译文】

孟子说："大王的不明智，没有什么不可理解的。即使有一种天下最容易生长的植物，见一天太阳，然后冻它十天，没有能够生长的。我见到大王的时候太少了，我一离开，那些给他'十日之寒'的谄媚之徒就去了，我就是能让他恢复一点智慧又有什么作用呢？比如下棋这种技艺，只是一种小技艺；但如果不专心致志地学习，也是学不会的。弈秋是全国棋术最高的人。让弈秋教两个人下棋。其中一个人专心致志，只听弈秋的话；另一个人虽然也在听，但心里却老是觉得有天鹅要飞来，想着拿起弓搭上箭去射它。这个人虽然与那个专心致志的人一起学习，却比不上那个人。是因为他的智力不如那个人吗？回答很明确：当然不是。"

Mencius said, "It is not to be wondered at that the King is not wise. Suppose there is the most easily growing plant under

Heaven. But if you let it have one day's genial heat, and then expose it for ten days to cold, it will not be able to grow. I rarely have a chance to see the King, and after I leave, there come all those who act upon him like the cold. Though I succeed in making him regain some wisdom, of what service is it? Now chess is actually a minor art, but if you don't concentrate well while learning it, you'll never be any good. Yi Qiu is the best player in the country, and let's say two men are learning from him. One man concentrates completely on everything Yi Qiu says, while the other one, while listening, is thinking about that goose over there and how he would draw his bow, adjust the string to the arrow, and shoot it. Although he is learning along with the other man, he will never be equal to him. Is this because his intelligence is inferior to another's? Of course not. "

仁，人心也；义，人路也。舍其路而弗由，放其心而不知求，哀哉！人有鸡犬放，则知求之；有放心，而不知求。学问之道无他，求其放心而已矣。

（《孟子》告子章句上）

【译文】

仁是人心最本质的特征；义是人应该走的道路。放弃了应该走的道路不走，丢失了最本质的特征却不知道寻求，真是悲哀啊！有的人鸡狗丢失了倒知道去找，本心丢失了却不知道去寻求。学问的关键不是别的，就是把那失去了的本心找回来罢了。

Benevolence is the essence of man's original heart – mind, and uprightness is the path man ought to follow. To abandon the true path and not follow it, or to lose the essence of heart – mind and not know enough to seek it, this is a pity indeed! When men's chickens and dogs are lost, they know to seek for them, but they lose their original heart – mind, and do not know to seek for it. The kernel of learning is nothing else but to seek for the lost mind.

羿之教人射，必志于彀；学者亦必志于彀。大匠诲人，必以规矩；学者亦必以规矩。

（《孟子》告子章句上）

【译文】

羿教人射箭，一定要把弓拉满，学射箭的人也一定要把弓拉满才行。高明的工匠教人一定遵循原则，学的人也一定要遵循原则才行。

Yi, in teaching men archery, made it a rule to draw the bow to the full, and his pupils also did the same. A master craftsman, in teaching others, is bound to observe principles, and his pupils must do the same.

曹交问曰："人皆可以为尧舜，有诸？"孟子曰："然。""交闻文王十尺，汤九尺，今交九尺四寸以长，食粟而已，如何则可？"

曰："奚有于是？亦为之而已矣。有人于此，力不能胜一匹雏，则为无力人矣；今曰举百钧，则为有力人矣。然则举乌获之任，是亦为乌获而已矣。夫人岂以不胜为患哉？弗为耳。徐行后长者谓之弟，疾行先长者谓之不弟。夫徐行者，岂人所不能哉？所不为也。尧舜之道，孝弟而已矣。子服尧之服，诵尧之言，行尧之行，是尧而已矣；子服桀之服，诵桀之言，行桀之行，是桀而已矣。"

曰："交得见于邹君，可以假馆，愿留而受业于门。"

曰："夫道，若大路然，岂难知哉？人病不求耳。子归而求之，有余师。"

（《孟子》告子章句下）

【译文】

曹交问道："人人都可以成为尧舜，有这种可能吗？"

孟子说："有。"

曹交说："我听说文王身高一丈，汤身高九尺，如今我身高九尺四寸多，却除了吃饭不会别的，我怎么做才能像说的那样呢？"

孟子说："身高有什么关系呢？只要像他那样去做就行了。有一个人，自以为连一只小鸡都提不起来，那他就是一个没有力气的人。要是他说要举起三千斤，那他就是想成为一个有力气的人。能举起古代大力士乌获所举的重量的，也就同样是乌获。人怎么能把不胜任作为忧患呢？只是不去做罢了。慢一点走，谦让长者叫做尊敬长者；快一点走，抢在长者之前叫做不尊敬长者。慢一点走难道是人做不到的吗？是不那样做而已。尧舜所走的道路，只不过就是父子之爱和兄弟之情之类的事罢了。你穿尧的衣服，说尧的话，做尧的事，你就是尧了。你穿桀的衣服，说桀的话，做桀的事，你就是桀了。"

曹交说："我准备去拜见邹君，向他借个住处，我愿意在先生这里做学生。"

孟子说："合乎义的道路就像宽广的大路一样，难道发现不了吗？人们的问题在于不去寻找。你回去自己寻找吧，老师多得很。"

Cao Jiao asked Mencius, "It is said, 'Everyone may be Yao and Shun.' Is it so?" Mencius replied, "It is."

Cao Jiao said, "I have heard that King Wen was two metres thirty centimetres in stature, and Tang two metres. Now I am two metres ten centimetres in height. But I can do nothing but eat. What am I to do to realize that saying?"

Mencius answered, "What has the stature to do with the matter? It all lies simply in acting as such. Here is a man, who believes he doesn't have enough strength to lift a chick, then he is a man of no strength. But if he says, 'I want to lift 500 kilograms' weight.' Then he wants to become a man of strength. And he who can lift the weight which Wu Huo, the ancient man of unusual strength, lifted is just another Wu Huo. Why should a man make a want of ability the subject of his grief? It is only that he will not do the thing. To walk a little slowly, keeping behind his elders, is to esteem his elders. To walk a little quickly and precede his elders, is to violate the duty of a younger brother. Is walking a little slowly what a man can't do? It is what he doesn't do. The course of Yao and Shun was simply the matter of filial benevolence and fraternal affection, and so forth. Wear the clothes of Yao, speak the words of Yao, and do the actions of Yao, and you will just be a Yao. And, if you wear the clothes of Jie, speak the words of Jie, and do the actions of Jie, you will just be a Jie."

Cao Jiao said, "I shall be having an interview with the monarch of Zou, asking him to lend me a house to lodge in. I wish to remain here, and receive instruction from you."

Mencius said, "The way of uprightness is like a broad

road. Is it difficult to find it? The problem with people is that they don't seek for it. If you go home and search for it, you will have abundance of teachers. "

教亦多术矣，予不屑之教诲也者，是亦教诲之而已矣。

（《孟子》告子章句下）

【译文】

教育有多种方法，我觉得一个人不纯洁所以不教他，这也是一种教育的方法。

There are many kinds of teaching techniques. I refuse to teach a man who is not chaste, but this is still a way of teaching.

仁言，不如仁声之入人深也。善政，不如善教之得民也。善政民畏之，善教民爱之；善政得民财，善教得民心。

（《孟子》尽心章句上）

【译文】

说仁德的话，不如因行仁德被百姓称颂那样感动人。颁布好的法律禁令，不如教育百姓为善那样得民心。好的法律禁令，百姓害怕；教育百姓为善，百姓喜爱。好的法律禁令能支配百姓的财物，教育百姓为善能得到民心。

Benevolent words do not touch people as much as a reputation for being benevolent. Promulgating good decree does not enjoy the ardent support of the people so much as nourishing them to be benevolent. The people fear good decree，but they love good instructions. Good decree can allocate the people's wealth，while good instructions gain their hearts.

君子之所以教者五：有如时雨化之者，有成德者，有达才者，有答问者，有私淑艾者。此五者，君子之所以教也。

（《孟子》尽心章句上）

【译文】

有道德的人教育人的方法有五种：有像及时雨一样启迪人的；有培养品德的；有培养才能的；有解答疑问的；有感化他人使他们模仿的。这五种，就是有道德的人教育人的方法。

The virtuous man teaches in five ways. There are some on whom his influence descends like timely rain. There are some whose virtue he perfects, and some of whose talents he assists the development. There are some whose questions he answers. There are some who privately cultivate and correct themselves. These are the ways in which the virtuous man teaches.

公孙丑曰："道则高矣，美矣，宜若登天然，似不可及也。何不使彼为可几及而日孳孳也？"

孟子曰："大匠不为拙工改废绳墨，羿不为拙射变其彀率。君子引而不发，跃如也。中道而立，能者从之。"

（《孟子》尽心章句上）

【译文】

公孙丑说："道倒是很高很好的，但就像登天一样，似乎高不可攀。为什么不使它成为可以攀及的因而叫人每天都去勤勉努力呢？"

孟子说："高明的工匠不因为拙劣的工人而改变或者废弃规矩，羿也绝不因为拙劣的射手而改变拉满弓的标准。有道德的人教人像只是张满了弓却不放箭，但怎样放箭已经很清楚了。他恰到好处地做出样子，有能力的人能学习他。"

Gong Sun Chou said: "Your principles are surely lofty and good, but they are too high to be reached, to learn them may well be likened to ascending the heavens. Why not make them attainable so that people will keep trying every day?" Mencius said, "A master craftsman does not alter or abandon principles for the sake of a clumsy workman. Yi did not charge his rule for drawing the bow for the sake of a clumsy archer. The virtuous man draws the bow, but does not discharge the arrow. Yet how to shoot an arrow is perfectly clear. He does just right for the purpose of demonstration. Those who are capable can follow him."

公都子曰："滕更之在门也，若在所礼。而不答，何也?"孟子曰："挟贵而问，挟贤而问，挟长而问，挟有勋劳而问，挟故而问，皆所不答也。滕更有二焉。"

（《孟子》尽心章句上）

【译文】

公都子说："滕更向先生学习，似乎应该在以礼相待之列，可是先生却不回答他的问题，为什么呢?"孟子说："倚仗着自己的权势来发问，倚仗着自己的才能来发问，倚仗着自己的年长来发问，倚仗着自己有功劳来发问，倚仗着自己是老交情来发问，都是我所不回答的。滕更有这五种中的两种。"

Gong Du Zi said, "When Teng Geng made his appearance in your school, it seemed that he should be treated with due respect, but you didn't answer his questions. Why was that?" Mencius said, "One who asks questions presuming on his rank, his ability, his seniority, his merits, or long-standing friendship, I will not answer. In Teng Geng's case two of these apply."

尽信书，则不如无书。吾于武成，取二三策而已矣。仁人无敌于天下。以至仁伐至不仁，而何其血之流杵也？

（《孟子》尽心章句下）

【译文】

完全相信书，那还不如没有书。我对于《尚书》中《武成》这一篇，就只相信其中的两三页罢了。仁德的人在天下没有敌手。以周武王这样极为仁德的人去讨伐商纣这样极不仁的人，怎么会使血流得可以漂起木棒呢？

It would be better to be without books than to give entire credit to them. In the "Completion of the War," I am only convinced of the content of two or three pages. The benevolent man has no enemy under Heaven. When King Wu, one of the most benevolent men, engaged Zhou, one of the most opposite, how could the blood of the people have flowed till it floated sticks?

梓匠轮舆，能与人规矩，不能使人巧。

(《孟子》尽心章句下)

【译文】

能工巧匠能教给别人规矩，但不能教会别人技巧。

Skilled craftsmen may impart rules and laws to others, but can't make them skilful in the use of them.

贤者以其昭昭，使人昭昭；今以其昏昏，使人昭昭。

(《孟子》尽心章句下)

【译文】

在古代，贤人先使自己明白，然后才去使别人明白；今天的人则是自己都没有搞清楚，却想去使别人明白。

Anciently, men of virtue and talents first made themselves enlightened, then they made others enlightened. Nowadays, people, while they are themselves in darkness, try to make others enlightened.

孟子之滕，馆于上宫。有业屦于牖上，馆人求之弗得。

或问之曰："若是乎从者之廋也？"曰："子以是为窃屦来与？"

曰："殆非也。""夫予之设科也，往者不追，来者不拒。苟以是心至，斯受之而已矣。"

（《孟子》尽心章句下）

【译文】

孟子到了滕国，住在上宫。有一只没织完的草鞋放在窗台上，可开旅馆的人找不着它了。

有人问孟子："是不是跟你来的人把它藏起来了？"孟子说："你认为他们是为了偷草鞋而来的吗？"

曰："大概不是。不过先生开设课程，走了的不追查，来的人不拒绝。只要是怀着学习的心愿来的，就全部接收。"

When Mencius went to Teng, he was lodged in the Upper palace. A straw sandal in the process of making had been placed there in a window, and when the keeper of the place came to look for it, he could not find it.

Someone asked Mencius, "Did your followers pilfer it?"

Mencius replied, "Do you think that they came here to pilfer the straw sandal?" The man said, "I apprehend not. But you, sir, having arranged to give lessons, you do not bother about those who leave, and you do not reject those who come to you. If they come with the mind to learn, you receive them without any more ado."

孟子语录

The Quotations by Mencius

修身

On Self-cultivation

☰

　　"告子曰：'不得于言，勿求于心；不得于心，勿求于气。'不得于心，勿求于气，可；不得于言，勿求于心，不可。夫志，气之帅也；气，体之充也。夫志至焉，气次焉。故曰：'持其志，无暴其气。'"

　　"既曰'志至焉，气次焉'，又曰'持其志无暴其气'者，何也？"

　　曰："志壹则动气，气壹则动志也。今夫蹶者趋者，是气也，而反动其心。"

　　"敢问夫子恶乎长？"

　　曰："我知言，我善养吾浩然之气。"

　　"敢问何谓浩然之气？"

　　曰："难言也。其为气也，至大至刚，以直养而无害，则塞于天地之间。其为气也，配义与道；无是，馁也。是集义所生者，非义袭而取之也。行有不慊于心，则馁矣。我故曰，告子未尝知义，以其外之也。必有事焉而勿正，心勿忘，勿助长也。无若宋人然：宋人有闵其苗之不长而揠之者，芒芒然归。谓其人曰：'今日病矣，予助苗长矣。'其子趋而往视之，苗则槁矣。天下之不助苗长者寡矣。以为无益而舍之者，不耘苗者也；助之长者，揠苗者也。非徒无益，而又害之。"

　　"何谓知言？"

　　曰："诐辞知其所蔽，淫辞知其所陷，邪辞知其所离，遁辞知其所穷。生于其心，害于其政；发于其政，害于其事。"

　　　　　　　　　　　　　　　　（《孟子》公孙丑章句上）

【译文】

"告子说，'不符合正确学说的话，舍弃即可，不必从内心中去寻找原因。不能获得内心的平静的事，不要为它使用自己的气力。'不能获得本心的平静的事，不要为它使用自己的气力，这么说是可以的。因为不符合正确的学说，就不从内心中去寻找原因，这是不对的。应该用志向引导生命的活力——气。气使身体充斥生命的活力。志向是最重要的，生命力还在其次。所以说，'要把握自己的志向，不要滥用自己的气力。'"

公孙丑问，"你刚才说，'志向是最重要的，生命力还在其次。'又说，'要把握自己的志向，不要滥用自己的气力。'这是为什么？"

孟子说："志向专注在什么事情上生命力就会集中到什么事情上；生命力集中在什么事情上，志向就在哪里。跑或跳这类事，虽然直接与气有关，但是能影响人的心意。"

公孙丑问，"请问先生擅长什么？"

孟子说："我善于辨别言论。我善于养护我义无反顾的生命之气。"

公孙丑问，"请问什么叫义无反顾的生命之气？"

孟子说："这难以用语言说明。它是生命力，是行善的动力，它的力量强大。顺其自然地养护它，不加以伤害，它就能使天地之间的事变得完美。作为生命力，它服务于义和道。没有它，人就会失去行善的力量。人身上的这种气是由

正义的行为积累产生的，不是通过偶然的正义行为所能得到
的。只要做一件有愧本心的事，这种气就削弱了。所以我
说，告子不懂得义，以为它不存在于内心之中。一定要做正
义的事，但不能强求培养这种气。心里时时想着它，但不能
违背规律培养它。不能像那个宋国人一样。宋国有一个担心
他的禾苗长不快而拔苗助长的人。得意地回到家里，对家人
说：'今天累坏了！我帮着禾苗长高了。'他的儿子赶快跑到
田里看，禾苗都枯萎了。实际上天下不拔苗助长培养这种气
的人很少。认为培养这种气的工作没有益处而舍弃的人，就
像种地不除草的人。而违背规律培养的人，就像拔苗助长的
人，不但没有好处，反而损害了它。"

公孙丑问，"什么叫善于辨别言论呢？"

孟子说："对不公道的言论，知道被遮蔽之处。对过分
的言论，知道它沉溺之处。对不合正道的言论，知道它偏离
正道的原因。对躲闪的言论，知道它理屈词穷之处。这些言
词从心中产生，就会在政治上造成危害。如果在政务中实
行，会对各项事业造成危害。"

"Gao said, 'What you do not obtain from the doctrines, do
not seek for it in the mind. If something disturbs the peace in
the mind, do not use your vigor for it. ' 'If something disturbs
the peace in the mind, do not use your vigor for it. ' This is correct. 'What you do not obtain from the doctrines, do not seek
for it in the mind. ' This is incorrect. One should guide his vig-

or with his will. Vigor animates the body. One's will is the most vital, vigor is the second. When the will arrives somewhere, vigor follows there. So it is said, 'Retain the upright will. Don't misuse the vigor.'"

Gong Sun Chou asked, "Since you have already said, 'One should guide his vigor with his will. Vigor animates the body.' Why do you also say, 'Retain the upright will. Don't misuse the vigor'?"

Mencius said, "When the will is focused on one thing, vigor will concentrates on it. When the vigor is devoted to one thing, then the will is focused on it. Things like running and jumping, though most directly concerned with the vigor, they nevertheless have an effect on one's intention."

Gong Sun Chou said, "May I ask in what you excel, sir?"

Mencius said, "I understand whatever words I hear. I am good at nourishing my flooding vigor."

Chou pursued, "I venture to ask what you mean by your flooding vigor?"

Mencius replied, "It is difficult to describe it. This is vigor. It is the dynamic to do good works. It is exceedingly powerful. If it is nourished in accordance with its natural tendency, and inflicted no injury, it will make the situation between Heaven and earth perfect. Being vigor, it serves uprightness and justice. Without it, man is deprived of the dynamic to do good works. For a man it is created by the accumulation of upright deeds; it is not to be obtained by incidental acts of uprightness. If the original heart – mind does not feel complacency in the conduct, it becomes weakened. So I say Gao has never understood uprightness, because he thinks it something outside the heart. There must be the constant practice of uprightness, but it mustn't be done for the purpose of nourishing this flooding vigor. Make sure the mind is always preoccupied with it, but let there be no violation of its natural tendency.

"Let us not be like the man of Song. There was a man of Song, who was worried that his growing corn was not longer, so he pulled it up. Having done this, he returned home, looking very pleased, and said to his wife and son, "I am tired today. I have been helping the corn to grow long. " His son ran to look at it, and found the corn all withered. There are few who don't do things as if they were assisting the corn to grow long. Some indeed consider nourishing this flooding vigor of no benefit to them, and let it alone. They are like the man doesn't weed his corn. Those who assist it to grow are like the man who pulled out his corn. What they do is not only of no benefit to this flooding vigor, but it also injures it. "

Gong Sun Chou asked, "What do you mean by saying that you understand whatever words you hear?"

Mencius replied, "When words are unfair, I know how the

mind of the speaker is clouded over. When words are extrava-gant, I know how the mind's indulgence. When words are all-depraved, I know how the mind has departed from the correct path. When words are ambiguous, I know how the mind is at its wit's end. These are weeds growing in the mind; they do in-jury to government, and, displayed in the government, are harmful to the conduct of affairs. "

子路，人告之以有过则喜。禹闻善言则拜。大舜有大焉，善与人同。舍己从人，乐取于人以为善。耕、稼、陶、渔以至为帝，无非取于人者。取诸人以为善，是与人为善者也。故君子莫大乎与人为善。

（《**孟子**》公孙丑章句上）

【译文】

子路，别人指出他的过错，他就因为有了机会改正而高兴。大禹听到有教益的话，就给说话的人行礼。伟大的舜帝就更加杰出，他把天下的善当做所有人的财富。舍弃自己的缺点，学习别人的优点，乐于吸取别人的长处来提高自己善良的品德。从他种地、做陶器、捕鱼一直到做帝王，他没有哪个时候不向别人学习。学习别人的优点来提高自己善良的品德，就是帮助别人行善。有道德的人最优秀的特征就是帮助天下的人行善。

When someone told Zi Lu that he had a fault, he was pleased to have the opportunity of correcting himself. When Yu heard good words, he bowed to the speaker. The great Shun surpassed even these men. He regarded virtue as the common property of all people under Heaven, overcoming his shortcomings to learn the merits of others, and taking delight in learning from others to develop his benevolence. From the time when he did farm work, made pottery, and was a fisherman, to the time when he became emperor, he never stopped learning from others. To learn from others to develop one's benevolence is to help others do good works. There is no attribute of the virtuous man greater than his helping men to practice benevolence.

吾闻之也：有官守者，不得其职则去；有言责者，不得其言则去。我无官守，我无言责也，则吾进退，岂不绰绰然有余裕哉？

（《孟子》公孙丑章句下）

【译文】

我听说过：有官位的人，如果无法尽其职责就应该辞职不干；有责任进言的人，如果进言不被听取，就应该辞职不干。我没有官位，没有进言的责任，那我的去留，不是有非常宽松的余地吗？

I have heard that he who is in charge of an office, when he is prevented from fulfilling his duties, ought to take his departure, and that he who has the responsibility to remonstrate with the sovereign, when he finds his words unattended to, ought to do the same. But I am in charge of no office; on me devolves no duty of speaking out my opinion. May not I therefore act freely and without any constraint, either in going forward or in retiring?

孟子为卿于齐，出吊于滕，王使盖大夫王驩为辅行。王驩朝暮见，反齐滕之路，未尝与之言行事也。

公孙丑曰："齐卿之位，不为小矣；齐滕之路，不为近矣。反之而未尝与言行事，何也？"

曰："夫既或治之，予何言哉？"

（《孟子》公孙丑章句下）

【译文】

孟子在齐国做卿相，奉命到滕国去吊唁，齐王派盖的地方官王驩为副使。王驩和孟子整天在一起，往返在齐、滕两国的路上，孟子却没有和他谈论政事。

公孙丑问："卿相的官位，不算小了；齐、滕两国之间的路，不算近了。往返一次却不和王驩谈论政事，这是为什么？"

孟子说："公务已有人办理，我还说什么呢？"

Mencius, occupying the position of minister in Qi, went on a mission of condolence to Teng. The King of Qi sent Wang Huan, the governor of Ge, as assistant – commissioner. Wang Huan waited upon Mencius all day long, traveling between Qi and Teng, but Mencius never spoke to him about the government affairs.

Gong Sun Chou asked Mencius, "The position of minister in Qi is not a small one; the road from Qi to Teng is not short. How was it that during all the way there and back, you never spoke to Wang Huan about the government affairs?"

Mencius replied, "There are officers who administer them. What had I to speak?"

　　燕人畔。王曰:"吾甚惭于孟子。"

　　陈贾曰:"王无患焉。王自以为与周公,孰仁且智?"王曰:"恶! 是何言也?"

　　曰:"周公使管叔监殷,管叔以殷畔。知而使之,是不仁也;不知而使之,是不智也。仁智,周公未之尽也,而况于王乎? 贾请见而解之。"见孟子问曰:"周公何人也?"

　　曰:"古圣人也。"曰:"使管叔监殷,管叔以殷畔也,有诸?"曰:"然。"

　　曰:"周公知其将畔而使之与?"曰:"不知也。"

　　"然则圣人且有过与?"

曰："周公，弟也；管叔，兄也。周公之过，不亦宜乎？且古之君子，过则改之；今之君子，过则顺之。古之君子，其过也，如日月之食，民皆见之；及其更也，民皆仰之。今之君子，岂徒顺之，又从为之辞。"

（《孟子》公孙丑章句下）

【译文】

燕国人群起反抗齐国。齐王说："我对孟子感到非常惭愧。"

陈贾说："大王不要难过。在仁和智的方面，大王和周公比较，谁强一些？"

齐王说："唉！这是什么话？"

陈贾说："周公让管叔监督殷国，管叔却率领殷人造反。知道这一结果还派他去，是不仁；不知道这一结果派他去，是不智。仁和智，连周公都没能完全做到，何况大王呢？我愿意去向孟子解释。"陈贾去见孟子，问："周公是怎样的人？"

孟子回答："古代的圣人。"

陈贾说："周公让管叔监督殷国，管叔却率领殷人造反。有这事吗？"

孟子回答："有。"

陈贾问："周公是知道这一结果还偏要派他去吗？"

孟子回答："周公不会预见得到。"

陈贾问："这么说，圣人也会有过错吗？"

孟子回答："周公是弟弟。管叔是哥哥。周公这种错误不也合乎情理吗？而且，古代有道德的人有了错误就改正。现在的人，有了错误就将错就错。古代有道德的人的错误就像日蚀月蚀一样，百姓们都看得清楚。当他改正的时候，百姓们都仰慕他。现在的人，有了错误不但将错就错，还编一套假道理来辩解。"

The people of Yen rallied together to rebel against Qi. The King of Qi said, "I feel quite ashamed when I think of Mencius. "

Chen Jia said to him, "Let not Your Majesty be grieved. Whether do Your Majesty consider yourself or the Duke of Zhou the more benevolent and wise?"

The King said, "Oh! What words are those?"

Chen Jia said, "The Duke of Zhou appointed Guan Shu to supervise Yin, but Guan Shu led the people of Yin to rebel. Knowing this would happen, he still appointed Guan Shu, then he was not benevolent. Not knowing this would happen, he appointed him, then he was not wise. If the Duke of Zhou was not completely benevolent and wise, let alone Your Majesty? I beg to go and see Mencius, and explain it to him. "

Chen Jia accordingly saw Mencius, and asked him, "What kind of man was the Duke of Zhou?" "An ancient sage. " Mencius answered.

Chen Jia said, "Is it the fact, that the Duke of Zhou appointed Guan Shu to supervise Yin, but Guan Shu led the people of Yin to rebel?"

Mencius said, "It is."

Chen Jia said, "Did the Duke of Zhou know that he would rebel, and still appointed him to that office?"

Mencius said, "He couldn't predict it."

Chen Jia said, "So even a sage can make a mistake?"

Mencius said, "The Duke of Zhou was the younger brother. Guan Shu was his elder brother. Didn't the mistake of Duke of Zhou stand to reason? Moreover, if the ancient made mistakes, they corrected them. The people today, when they make mistakes, leave the mistakes uncorrected and make the best of it. The mistakes of the ancient were like eclipses of the sun and moon. All the people witnessed them, and when they had corrected them, all the people looked up to them. People today not only leave the mistakes uncorrected and make the best of it, but also try to explain it away."

夫天，未欲平治天下也；如欲平治天下，当今之世，舍我其谁也？吾何为不豫哉？

（《孟子》公孙丑章句下）

【译文】

现在上天大概还不想让天下太平。如果上天想让天下太平，在当今这个时代，除了我，还有谁能完成这个任务呢？我为什么不愉快呢？

Maybe Heaven does not yet wish that the land under Heaven should enjoy peace and tranquility. If it wished this, who is there besides me to bring it about? Why should I be unpleasant?

滕文公为世子，将之楚，过宋而见孟子。孟子道性善，言必称尧舜。

世子自楚反，复见孟子。孟子曰："世子疑吾言乎？夫道一而已矣。成䁲谓齐景公曰：'彼丈夫也，我丈夫也，吾何畏彼哉？'颜渊曰：'舜何人也？予何人也？有为者亦若是。'公明仪曰：'文王我师也，周公岂欺我哉？'

今滕，绝长补短，将五十里也，犹可以为善国。书曰：'若药不瞑眩，厥疾不瘳。'"

（《孟子》滕文公章句上）

【译文】

滕文公还是太子的时候，要到楚国去，经过宋国时拜访了孟子。孟子给他讲人的本性是善良的，举例的时候总提到尧舜。

太子从楚国回来，又来拜访孟子。孟子说："殿下不相信我的话吗？人间正道都是一样的。成睍对齐景公说：'有德有才的人是一个男子汉，我也是一个男子汉，我为什么要敬畏他呢？'颜渊说：'舜是人，我也是人，有作为的人也会像舜那样。'公明仪说：'我把文王作为自己的老师；周公难道会比我强吗？'现在的滕国，假如把疆土截长补短也有将近五十里吧。还可以治理成一个好国家。《尚书》说'如果药不能使人头昏眼花，那病是不会痊愈的。'"

When the Duke Wen of Teng was crown prince, he had to go to Chu, he went by way of Song and visited Mencius. Mencius discoursed to him how the original nature of man is good, and when giving examples, always mentioned Yao and Shun.

When the crown prince was returning from Chu, he again visited Mencius. Mencius said to him, "Your Highness doubt my words? The correct path is the same.

"Cheng Jian said to Duke Jing of Qi, 'The virtuous and a-ble men were men. I am a man. Why should I stand in awe of them?' Yan Yuan said, 'Shun was a man. I am a man. He who is able to develop his ability to the full will also become such as he was.' Gong Ming Yi said, 'I take King Wen for my teacher. How should the Duke of Zhou exceed me?' The current state of Teng, taking its length with its breadth, will amount to twenty miles. It is still sufficient to make a good state. It is said in the Book of History, 'If medicine does not raise a commotion in the patient, his disease will not be cured by it.'"

枉己者，未有能直人者也。

（《孟子》滕文公章句下）

【译文】

自己不正直的人从来没有能让别人正直的。

Never has a man who has bent himself been able to make others straight.

居天下之广居，立天下之正位，行天下之大道。得志与民由之，不得志独行其道。富贵不能淫，贫贱不能移，威武不能屈。此之谓大丈夫。

（《孟子》滕文公章句下）

【译文】

住在天下最宽广的住宅——仁里，站在天下最正确的位置——礼上，走在天下最光明的大道——义上。得志的时候，把道德传授给百姓；不得志的时候，独自坚守自己的原则。富贵不能使他的心摇摆，贫贱不能改变他的节操，威武不能挫伤他的志向。这样才叫做大丈夫。

To dwell in the broadest house under Heaven— benevolence，to stand in the most correct position under Heaven — etiquette，and to walk in the brightest path under Heaven — uprightness. When his wishes were to be realized，he passes on virtue to people. When he is unable to realized his wishes，he stands to his principle alone. Riches and honour can't make his heart sway. Poverty and destitution can't modify his integrity. Force can't subdue his will. Then he can be called a true man.

公都子曰："外人皆称夫子好辩，敢问何也？"

孟子曰："予岂好辩哉？予不得已也。"

（《孟子》滕文公章句下）

【译文】

公都子曰："外人都说先生喜欢巧辩，是这样吗？"

孟子曰："我哪里是喜欢巧辩？我是不得已。"

Gong Du Zi asked，"Outsiders all say that you are fond of argument. Is that true?"

Mencius answered, "I am not fond of argument. I simply have no alternative."

离娄之明，公输子之巧，不以规矩，不能成方员；师旷之聪，不以六律，不能正五音；尧舜之道，不以仁政，不能平治天下。

（《孟子》离娄章句上）

【译文】

即使有离娄那样好的视力，鲁班那样高超的技巧，如果不用圆规和角尺，也不能准确地画出圆形和方形；即使有师旷样好的听力，如果不用六律，也不能校正五音；即使有尧舜的学说，如果不以仁政为法度，也不能治理好天下。

The power of vision of Li Lou, and skill of hand of Lu Ban, without the compass and angle square, could not form circles and squares. The acute ear of Shi Kuang, without the pitch – tubes, could not determine correctly the five notes. The principles of Yao and Shun, without a benevolent government, could not govern the land under Heaven well.

规矩，方员之至也；圣人，人伦之至也。

（《孟子》离娄章句上）

【译文】

圆规和角尺能画出最完美的圆形和方形；在圣人身上，人和人之间的必然关系体现得最完美。

The compass and angle square produce perfect circles and squares. With the sages, the inexorable relations between individuals are perfectly exhibited.

爱人不亲反其仁，治人不治反其智，礼人不答反其敬。行有不得者，皆反求诸己，其身正而天下归之。诗云："永言配命，自求多福。"

（《孟子》离娄章句上）

【译文】

以仁爱对待别人却得不到别人的亲近，那就应该反问自己的仁爱是否还不够；管理别人却不能够管理好，那就应该反问自己的智慧是否还不够；礼貌待人却得不到别人相应的礼貌，那就应该反问自己的礼貌是否还不够。凡是行为得不到预期的效果，都应该反过来检查自己。自要自身端正了，连天下的人都会归服。《诗经》上说："永远要遵循天命，幸福是自己求得的。"

If a man treats others out of pure humanity, and there is no repayment for his kindness, let him turn inwards and examine himself to see if his benevolence is insufficient. If he attempts to govern others with order, and his government is unsuccessful, let him turn inwards and examine himself to see if his wisdom is deficient. If he treats others with courtesy, and they do not return his courtesy, let him turn inwards and examine himself to see if his politeness is inadequate. When our actions do not achieve the desired results, we must turn inwards, and examine ourselves. When a man's person is correct, he can make the people under Heaven yield. It is said in the Book of Poetry,

"Always follow the mandate of Heaven,

For happiness is in your own hands."

人有恒言，皆曰"天下国家"。天下之本在国，国之本在家，家之本在身。

（《孟子》离娄章句上）

【译文】

人们有句口头语，都说"天下，国，家"。天下的基础是国，国的基础是家，家的基础是个人。

People have this common saying, "The land under Heaven, the state, the family." The root of the land under Heaven is in the state. The root of the state is in the family. The root of the family is in the members of it.

存乎人者，莫良于眸子。眸子不能掩其恶。胸中正，则眸子了焉；胸中不正，则眸子眊焉。听其言也，观其眸子，人焉廋哉？

（《孟子》离娄章句上）

【译文】

观察一个人，再没有比观察他的眼睛更好的了。眼睛不能掩盖一个人内心的丑恶。内心正直，眼睛就明亮；内心不正直，眼睛就昏暗。听一个人说话的时候，注意观察他的眼睛，他的善恶能往哪里隐藏呢？

There is no better way to observe a man than looking at the pupil of his eye. The pupil can't be used to hide a man's wickedness. If within the breast all be correct, the pupil is bright. If within the breast all be not correct, the pupil is dull. Listen to a man's words and look at the pupil of his eye. How can a man conceal his character?

恭者不侮人，俭者不夺人。侮夺人之君，惟恐不顺焉，恶得为恭俭？恭俭岂可以声音笑貌为哉？

（《孟子》离娄章句上）

【译文】

恭敬别人的人不会侮辱人，自己节俭的人不会掠夺别人。侮辱别人掠夺别人的君王，惟恐别人不顺从自己，怎么会恭敬别人和自己节俭呢？恭敬别人和自己节俭难道是能用好听的声音和笑脸做出来的吗？

Those who respect people never humiliate others. Those who are economical never plunder others. The King who treats men with despite and plunders them, is only afraid that they are not obedient to him. How can he respect people or be economical? How can respectfulness and economy be made out of pleasant tones of the voice, and a smiling face?

有不虞之誉，有求全之毁。

（《孟子》离娄章句上）

【译文】

会有过度的赞誉；也会有求全责备造成的损害。

There are cases of praise which could not be expected; there are cases where harm is caused by demanding perfection.

人之易其言也，无责而矣。

（《孟子》离娄章句上）

【译文】

人随便讲话是因为可以不受责备。

Men's being ready with their tongues arises simply from their not having been reproved.

人之患在好为人师。

（《孟子》离娄章句上）

【译文】

人的一种大毛病是喜欢对别人指手画脚。

One of man's major drawbacks is being fond of teaching others.

非礼之礼，非义之义，大人弗为。

（《孟子》离娄章句下）

【译文】

不出于真心的礼节，不出于真心的正义行为，有道德的人不做这样的事。

Acts of etiquette which are not from the depth of the heart, and acts of uprightness which are not from the depth of the heart, the virtuous man does not do.

人有不为也，而后可以有为。

（《孟子》离娄章句下）

【译文】

一个人要首先决定不去做什么事，才能义无反顾地去做该做的事。

A man must first decide on what he will not do, and then he is able to act with vigour in what he ought to do.

仲尼不为已甚者。

（《孟子》离娄章句下）

【译文】

孔子不做超出本分的事。

Confucius did not do things beyond his obligation.

徐子曰："仲尼亟称于水，曰：'水哉，水哉！'何取于水也？"

孟子曰："原泉混混，不舍昼夜。盈科而后进，放乎四海，有本者如是，是之取尔。苟为无本，七八月之间雨集，沟浍皆盈；其涸也，可立而待也。故声闻过情，君子耻之。"

（《孟子》离娄章句下）

【译文】

徐子说："孔子几次称赞水，说：'水啊！水啊！'他觉得水有什么可取之处呢？"

孟子说："水从源泉里滚滚涌出，日夜不停。它把所有低洼处灌满，然后继续向前，流进大海。有源泉的就是这样。孔子所取的就是泉水的这种特点。如果水没有这种永不枯竭的源泉，就会像七八月的雨水集聚一样，虽然可以灌满田间沟渠。但是很快就会干涸。所以，名声超过本质，有道德的人会对这种情况感到羞耻。"

Xu Zi said, "Confucius praised water time and again, saying, 'Oh water! Oh water!' What did he find in water to praise?"

Mencius replied, "Water gushes from its source, day and night and without stop. It fills up every pit, and then advances, flowing onto the sea. Such is water having a source. It was this which he found in it to praise. Suppose that the water has no source. As in the case in the seventh and eighth month when the rain falls abundantly, the channels in the fields are all filled, but they will dry up again shortly. So a perfect gentleman is ashamed of a reputation beyond his merits."

西子蒙不洁，则人皆掩鼻而过之。虽有恶人，齐戒沐浴，则可以祀上帝。

（《孟子》离娄章句下）

【译文】

就是西施身上沾上肮脏的东西，别人也都会捂着鼻子走过去。即使是一个相貌丑陋的人，只要斋戒沐浴，也同样可以祭祀上帝。

If Xi Shi had been covered with a filthy head – dress, people would have stopped their noses in passing her. If a man were ugly, yet if he had fasted and bathed, he might be able to sacrifice to God.

储子曰："王使人瞯夫子，果有以异于人乎？"孟子曰："何以异于人哉？尧舜与人同耳。"

（《孟子》离娄章句下）

【译文】

储子说："大王派人来窥探先生，先生真和一般人不同吗？"孟子曰："我和别人有什么不同呢？尧和舜也和一般人一样。"

Chu Zi said to Mencius, "Sir, the King sent persons to spy upon you. Are you really different from other men?" Mencius answered, "How should I be different from other men? Yao and Shun were just the same as other men."

伯夷，目不视恶色，耳不听恶声。非其君不事，非其民不使。治则进，乱则退。横政之所出，横民之所止，不忍居也。

（《孟子》万章章句下）

【译文】

伯夷，眼睛不看不好的东西，耳朵不听不好的声音。不是他理想的君王，不去侍奉；不是他理想的百姓，不去支使。天下太平就出来做官，天下混乱就告退隐居。施行暴政的国家，居住暴民的地方，他都不忍心居住在那里。

Bo Yi would not allow his eyes to look on a bad sight, nor his ears to listen to a bad sound. He would not serve a sovereign if he is not his ideal sovereign, nor command people if they are not his ideal people. When peace reigns over the land he took office, and on the occurrence of confusion he retired. He could not bear to dwell in a state under tyrannical rule, or in a place among mob.

万章问曰："敢问友。"

孟子曰："不挟长，不挟贵，不挟兄弟而友。友也者，友其德也，不可以有挟也。孟献子，百乘之家也，有友五人焉：乐正裘、牧仲，其三人，则予忘之矣。献子之与此五人者友也，无献子之家者也。此五人者，亦有献子之家，则不与之友矣。非惟百乘之家为然也。虽小国之君亦有之。费惠公曰：'吾于子思，则师之矣；吾于颜般，则友之矣；王顺、长息则事我者也。'非惟小国之君为然也，虽大国之君亦有之。晋平公之于亥唐也，入云则入，坐云则坐，食云则食。虽疏食菜羹，未尝不饱，盖不敢不饱也。然终于此而已矣。弗与共天位也，弗与治天职也，弗与食天禄也，士之尊贤者也，非王公之尊贤也。舜尚见帝，帝馆甥于贰室，亦飨舜，迭为宾主，是天子而友匹夫也。用下敬上，谓之贵贵；用上敬下，谓之尊贤。贵贵、尊贤，其义一也。"

（《孟子》万章章句下）

【译文】

万章问："请问交朋友的原则是什么？"

·孟子回答："不倚仗自己年龄大，不倚仗自己地位高，不倚仗兄弟的势力去交朋友。交朋友，是因为对方的品德去结交，不能倚仗什么。孟献子是拥有百辆车马的大夫，他有五位朋友：乐正裘、牧仲，其余三位，我忘记了。孟献子与这五人交朋友，心中没有想着自己是大夫；这五人，如果心中想着孟献子是大夫，就不会与他交朋友了。不仅有百辆车马的大夫有这样的，小国的国君也有这样的。费惠公说：'我把子思当做老师；我把颜般当做朋友；至于王顺和长息，不过是为我办事的人罢了。'不仅小国的国君有这样的，就是大国的国君也有这样的。晋平公对待亥唐就这样。亥唐叫他进去就进去，叫他坐就坐，叫他吃就吃。虽然是糙米饭和菜汤，也吃饱了，因为不敢不吃饱。不过，晋平公也就是做到这一步而已。不同他一起共有官位，不同他一起治理政事，不同他一起享受俸禄，这只是一般士人尊敬有道德的人的态度，而不是王公对待有道德的人应有的态度。舜帝拜见尧帝，尧请他的这位女婿住在待客的宫邸。他请舜吃饭，舜也请他吃饭，二人互为主人和客人。这就是天子和百姓交朋

三 修身 On Self-cultivation

友的范例。地位低的人尊敬地位高的人，叫尊敬贵人；地位
高的人尊敬地位低的人，叫尊敬贤人。尊敬贵人和尊敬贤
人，道理都是一样的。"

Wan Zhang asked Mencius, "I venture to ask the principles
of friendship."

Mencius replied, "Friendship should be maintained without
any presumption on the ground of one's superior age, or position, or the influence of his brothers. Friendship with a man is
friendship with his virtue, and does not admit of assumptions of
superiority. Meng Xian Zi was the chief of a family of a hundred
chariots. He had five friends: Yue Zheng Qiu, Mu Zhong, and
three others whose names I have forgotten. Meng Xian Zi maintained friendship with those five men, and thought nothing a-
bout his family. If those five men had thought about his family,
they would not have maintained their friendship with him. Not
only has the chief of a family of a hundred chariots acted thus.
The same thing was exemplified by the sovereign of a small
state. The Duke Hui of Fei said, 'I treat Zi Si as my teacher,
and Yan Ban as my friend. As to Wang Shun and Chang Xi,
they serve me.' Not only has the sovereign of a small state acted thus. The same thing has been exemplified by the sovereign
of a large state. There was the Duke Ping of Jin with Hai
Tang: when Hai Tang told him to come into his house, he

came; when he told him to be seated, he sat; when he told him to eat, he ate. Although there was only coarse rice and soup of vegetables, but he ate his fill, not daring to do otherwise. But the Duke Ping of Jin stopped here and went no farther. He didn't call him to share office, or to administer any government affairs with him, or to partake salary. His conduct was but a scholar's honoring virtuous people, not the honoring them proper to a King or a Duke. Shun paid a formal visit to Yao, who lodged this son-in-law in the second palace. Yao invited Shun to dinner. Shun also invited Yao to dinner. Alternately, they were host or guest. Here was the sovereign maintaining friendship with a private man. Respect shown by inferiors to superiors is called respecting the noble. Respect shown by superiors to inferiors is called respecting the virtuous. The principle in each case is the same. "

立乎人之本朝，而道不行，耻也。

（《孟子》万章章句下）

【译文】

在别人的朝廷做官却不能实现自己的主张，这是耻辱。

When a scholar stands in other's court, and his principles

are not carried into practice, it is a shame to him.

孟子谓万章曰："一乡之善士，斯友一乡之善士；一国之善士，斯友一国之善士；天下之善士，斯友天下之善士。以友天下之善士为未足，又尚论古之人。颂其诗，读其书，不知其人，可乎？是以论其世也。是尚友也。"

（《孟子》万章章句下）

【译文】

孟子对万章说："在一个乡里行善的人，就要和这个乡里所有行善的人交朋友；在一个国家里行善的人，就要和这个国家里所有行善的人交朋友；在天下行善的人，就要和天下所有行善的人交朋友。如果和天下所有行善的人交朋友还不够，就上溯古代行善的人。读他们的诗，看他们的书，但不知道他们的为人处事，怎么可以呢？所以还要研究他们的事迹。这就是上溯历史和古人交朋友。"

Mencius said to Wan Zhang, "The man who does good works in a village should make friends of all those who do good works in the village. The man who does good works in a state should make friends of all those who do good works in the state. The man who does good works in the land under Heaven should make friends of all those who do good works in the land under Heaven. When he feels that his friendship with all the people who do good works in the land under Heaven is not sufficient to satisfy him, he may proceed to ascend to consider the men of antiquity. He can study their poems, and read their books. But he needs to know how they conducted themselves. So he must consider their history. This is to ascend and make friends of the men of antiquity."

生，亦我所欲也；义，亦我所欲也，二者不可得兼，舍生而取义者也。生亦我所欲，所欲有甚于生者，故不为苟得也；死亦我所恶，所恶有甚于死者，故患有所不辟也。

（《孟子》告子章句上）

【译文】

生命是我所追求的，正义也是我所追求的；如果不能两样都拥有，我就舍弃生命而坚持正义。生命是我想拥有的，但是还有比生命更让我想拥有的，所以我不愿意苟且偷生；死亡是我想躲避的，但是还有比死亡更让我想躲避的，所以我不会因为躲避死亡而逃避某些祸患。

I desire life, and I also desire uprightness. If I can't have both, I will give up life, and uphold uprightness. I desire life indeed, but there is that which I desire more than life, hence, I will not seek to possess it by any improper ways. I dislike death indeed, but there is that which I dislike more than death, hence, there are calamities I don't avoid.

今有无名之指，屈而不信，非疾痛害事也，如有能信之者，则不远秦楚之路，为指之不若人也。指不若人，则知恶之；心不若人，则不知恶，此之谓不知类也。

（《孟子》告子章句上）

【译文】

有人的无名指弯曲而不能伸直，虽然并不疼痛，也不妨碍做事情，但只要有人能使它伸直，就是要从秦国跑到楚国去，也不会嫌远，为的是无名指不如别人。无名指不如别人，就知道厌恶；心不如别人，却不知道厌恶。这叫做不知轻重。

Here is a man whose third finger is bent and can't be stretched out straight. It is not painful, nor does it incommode his business, and yet if there is one who can make it straight, he will not think the way from Qin to Chu far to go to him; because his finger is not as good as the fingers of other people. When a man's finger is not as good as those of other people, he knows to feel dissatisfaction, but if his mind is not like that of other people, he doesn't know to feel dissatisfaction. This is called "Ignorance of the relative importance of things."

拱把之桐梓，人苟欲生之，皆知所以养之者。至于身，而不知所以养之者，岂爱身不若桐梓哉？弗思甚也。

（《孟子》告子章句上）

【译文】

一两把粗的桐树和梓树，想要让它生长，都知道怎么去培育。对于自己却不知道怎样去培养，爱自己还不如爱桐树和梓树吗？真是太不会思考问题了。

Anybody who wishes to grow the paulownia or the catalpa, which may be grasped with both hands, knows by what means to cultivate them. In the case of their own persons, men do not know by what means to cultivate them. Is it to be supposed that their regard for their own persons is inferior to their regard for the paulownia or the catalpa? Their want of reflection is extreme.

耳目之官不思，而蔽于物，物交物，则引之而已矣。心之官则思，思则得之，不思则不得也。此天之所与我者，先立乎其大者，则其小者弗能夺也。此为大人而已矣。

（《孟子》告子章句上）

【译文】

　　眼睛耳朵这类器官不会思考，所以被外物所蒙蔽。这些处于物的水平上的东西一接触外物，便容易被吸引而去。心这个器官则有思考的能力，思考就知道外物的本质，不思考就不知道外物的本质。这种能力是上天赋予人类的。所以要先把心这个重要部分的作用确立起来，次要的部分就不会喧宾夺主了。这样就可以成为有道德的人了。

The organs such as the eye and the ear do not think, and they are easily led astray by external things. When these organs, which are things in nature, are exposed to external things, they are easily to be drawn away. The function of the mind is to think. By thinking, the nature of external things can be known. If one doesn't think, he won't be able to know it. The ability of thinking is bestowed upon us by Heaven. Therefore, we must first establish ourselves in the primary part, then the secondary part can't overshadow the primary. This is the essential to be a virtuous man.

　　有天爵者，有人爵者。仁义忠信，乐善不倦，此天爵也；

公卿大夫，此人爵也。古之人修其天爵，而人爵从之。今之人修其天爵，以要人爵；既得人爵，而弃其天爵，则惑之甚者也，终亦必亡而已矣。

（《孟子》告子章句上）

【译文】

有天赐的爵位，有人授的爵位。仁义忠信，不厌倦地乐于行善，这是天赐的爵位；公卿大夫，这是人授的爵位。古代的人修养天赐的爵位，水到渠成地获得人授的爵位。现在的人修养天赐的爵位，其目的就在于得到人授的爵位；一旦得到人授的爵位，便抛弃了天赐的爵位。这可真是糊涂得很啊！最终连人授的爵位也必定会失去。

There is the dignity granted by Heaven, and there is the dignity granted by man. Benevolence, uprightness, faithfulness, and sincerity, and a tireless delight in the practice of benevolence, these constitute the dignity granted by Heaven. To be a King, minister, or a senior official, this constitutes the dignity granted by man. The men of antiquity cultivated their heavenly dignity, and naturally obtained the dignity granted by man. The men of the present day cultivate their heavenly dignity in order to gain the dignity granted by man, and once they have that, they throw away the other. How delusional they are! For in the end they will lose the dignity granted by man as well.

任人有问屋庐子曰："礼与食孰重?"曰："礼重。"

"色与礼孰重?"曰："礼重。"

曰："以礼食，则饥而死；不以礼食，则得食，必以礼乎？亲迎，则不得妻；不亲迎，则得妻，必亲迎乎？"屋庐子不能对，明日之邹以告孟子。

孟子曰："于答是也何有？不揣其本而齐其末，方寸之木可使高于岑楼。金重于羽者，岂谓一钩金与一舆羽之谓哉？取食之重者，与礼之轻者而比之，奚翅食重？取色之重者，与礼之轻者而比之，奚翅色重？往应之曰：'紾兄之臂而夺之食，则得食；不紾，则不得食，则将紾之乎？踰东家墙而搂其处子，则得妻；不搂，则不得妻，则将搂之乎？'"

（《**孟子**》告子章句下）

【译文】

有个任国人问屋庐子说："礼和吃饭哪样重要?"屋庐子说："礼重要。"？那人问："娶妻和礼哪样重要?"

屋庐子说："礼重要。"

那人又问："如果非要符合礼节才吃饭，就只有饿死；不按照礼节吃饭，就可以得到吃的，那也一定要符合礼节才吃饭吗？如果非要符合礼制才娶妻，就娶不到妻子；不按照礼制娶妻，就可以娶到妻子，那也一定要符合礼制才娶妻吗？"

屋庐子不能回答，第二天就到邹国，把这些话告诉了孟子。

孟子说："回答这个问题有什么困难呢？如果不看基础的高低是否一致，只比较顶端，那么一块一寸见方的木头也可以高过巍峨的高楼。说黄金比羽毛重，难道是说一个衣带钩的黄金比一车羽毛重吗？拿有关吃的要紧事和有关礼的琐碎事比较，难道还不是吃重要？拿有关娶妻的要紧事和有关礼的琐碎事比较，难道还不是娶妻重要？你去这样答复他：'扭断哥哥的胳膊，夺走他的食物，就可以得到吃的；不扭断哥哥的胳膊，就没有吃的，那会去扭断吗？爬过东边人家的墙掠走他家的处女，就可以得到妻子；不掠夺，就得不到妻子，那会去掠夺吗？'"

A man of Ren asked Wu Lu Zi, "Is obeying the rules of etiquette, or eating, the more important?" Wu Lu Zi answered, "The obeying the rules of etiquette is the more important."

"Is marring a wife, or obeying the rules of etiquette, the more important?" Wu Lu Zi answered, "The obeying the rules of etiquette is the more important."

The man pursued, "If the result of eating only according to the rules of etiquette will be death by starvation, while by disregarding those rules one may get food, must he obey the rules of etiquette in such a case? If he proposes marriage only according to the rules of etiquette, he can't get married, while by disregarding those rules he may get married, must he obey the rules of etiquette in such a case?"

Wu Lu Zi was unable to find an answer, the next day he went to Zou, and told them to Mencius. Mencius said, "What difficulty is there in answering these questions? If you do not look at their foundations, but only put their tops on a level, a piece of wood an inch square may be made to be higher than the pinnacle of a high tower. It's said that gold is heavier than feathers. But does that saying have reference that a single clasp of gold is heavier than a wagon – load of feathers? If you take a case where the eating is of the utmost importance and obeying the rules of etiquette doesn't count for much, and compare them together, isn't eating the more important? And if you take a case where marring a wife is of the utmost importance and obeying the rules of etiquette doesn't count for much, and compare them together, isn't marring a wife the more important? Go and answer him this way, 'If, by twisting your elder brother's arm, taking what he is eating by force, you can get food for yourself. If you do not do so, you will not get anything to eat. Will you so twist his arm? If, by climbing over your neighbor's wall, and dragging away his virgin daughter, you can get a wife. If you do not do so, you will not be able to get a wife. Will you so drag her away?'"

孟子居邹，季任为任处守，以币交，受之而不报。处于平陆，储子为相，以币交，受之而不报。他日由邹之任，见季子；由平陆之齐，不见储子。屋庐子喜曰："连得闲矣。"

问曰："夫子之任见季子，之齐不见储子，为其为相与?"

曰："非也。书曰:'享多仪，仪不及物曰不享，惟不役志于享。'为其不成享也。"

屋庐子悦。或问之。屋庐子曰："季子不得之邹，储子得之平陆。"

（《孟子》告子章句下）

【译文】

孟子居住在邹国的时候，季任在任国摄政，派人送钱财来和孟子交朋友，孟子接受了但没作回报。孟子居住在平陆的时候，储子是相，派人送钱财来和孟子交朋友，孟子接受了但没作回报。过了一段时间孟子从邹国去任国，拜访了季子；从平陆到齐国，没去拜访储子。屋庐子高兴地说："我发现问题了。"

他问道："先生到了任国去拜访季子，到了齐国不去拜访储子，是因为储子只是相吗?"

孟子说："不是。《尚书》中说:'赠送礼物重要的是礼节，礼节不够礼物虽然多也只能叫做没有赠送，因为送礼物的人的心思没有用在这上面。'因为他没有完成赠送。"

屋庐子很高兴。有人问他。屋庐子说："季子不能亲自去邹国，而储子本可以亲自去平陆。"

When Mencius was residing in Zou, Ji Ren acted as regent in Ren. He sent people to present cash gift to Mencius to make friends with him. Mencius accepted, and made no repayment for it. When Mencius was dwelling in Ping Lu, Chu Zi was prime minister of the state. He sent people to present cash gift to Mencius to make friends with him. Mencius received in the same way. Later on, Mencius went from Zou to Ren, he paid Ji Ren a visit. But he didn't visit Chu Zi.

The disciple Wu Lu Zi beamed and said, "I see a contradiction."

He asked, "Sir, when you went to Ren, you visited Ji Ren; and when you went to Qi, you did not visit Chu Zi. Was it not because he is only the minister?"

Mencius replied, "No. It is said in the Book of History, 'In presenting a gift to someone, most depends on the etiquette. If the demonstrations of etiquette are not adequate, we say there is no offering, because the gift is not a token of regard.' Since the things so offered do not constitute an offering."

Wu Lu Zi was pleased, and when someone asked him what Mencius meant, he said, "Ji Ren could not go to Zou, but Chu Zi might have gone to Ping Lu."

君子不亮，恶乎执？

（《孟子》告子章句下）

【译文】

有地位的人不讲诚信，怎么能有操守呢？

If a gentleman have no faith, how can he take a firm hold of things?

陈子曰："古之君子何如则仕？"孟子曰："所就三，所去三。迎之致敬以有礼，言将行其言也，则就之；礼貌未衰，言弗行也，则去之。其次，虽未行其言也，迎之致敬以有礼，则就之；礼貌衰，则去之。其下，朝不食，夕不食，饥饿不能出门户。君闻之曰：'吾大者不能行其道，又不能从其言也，使饥饿于我土地，吾耻之。'周之，亦可受也，免死而已矣。"

（《孟子》告子章句下）

【译文】

陈子问："古代有道德的人怎样才出来做官？"孟子说："任职的情况有三种，辞职的情况也有三种。尊敬有礼地迎接他，说会按照他的话去做，就任职；礼节还在，但不按照他的话去做，就辞职。次一等的，虽然不按照他的话去做，但尊敬有礼地迎接他，就任职；礼节不在了，就辞职。最下

修身 On Self-cultivation

第七五页

等的，早晨没饭吃，晚上没饭吃，饥饿得不能走出家门。君
王听说了，说：'我不能实行他的学说，又不能按照他的话
去做，使得他在我的国土上挨饿，这是我的耻辱。'于是周
济他，这也可以接受，只是为了不饿死而已。"

Chen Zi said, "What were the principles on which perfect
gentlemen of ancient times took office?"

Mencius replied, "There were three cases in which they accepted office, and three in which they left it. If being received
with respect, and being told that the sovereigns would carry
their words into practice, then they took office. Afterwards,
although there was no remission in etiquette, but their words
were not carried into practice, then they would leave. The second case was that in which, though the sovereigns could not be
expected to carry their words into practice, yet being received
with respect, they took office. But afterwards, if there was a
remission in etiquette, they would leave. The last case was that
if the perfect gentleman had nothing to eat, either morning or
evening, and was so famished that he could not move out of his
door. If the sovereign, on hearing of his state, said, 'I am not
able to carry his doctrines into practice, neither am I able to follow his words, but I am ashamed to allow him to starve in my
country.' Consequently, the sovereign helped him with the offering of a post. The assistance in such a case might be accept-

ed，bit it's only for averting death."

天将降大任于斯人也，必先苦其心志，劳其筋骨，饿其体肤，空乏其身，行拂乱其所为，所以动心忍性，曾益其所不能。人恒过，然后能改；困于心，衡于虑，而后作；征于色，发于声，而后喻。入则无法家拂士，出则无敌国外患者，国恒亡。然后知生于忧患而死于安乐也。

（《孟子》告子章句下）

【译文】

上天要让某人去完成重大使命，一定先要让他的意志受到磨炼，使他的筋骨受到劳累，使他的身体忍饥挨饿，使他备受穷困之苦，做事总是不顺利。这样来激发他的内心深处，坚定他的本性，弥补他的缺点。人总是先犯错误，然后才能改正错误；心里感到困惑，想不出解决问题的办法，这样才能奋发而起；这会表现在自己脸上，体现在说的话里，这样就能影响他人。一个国家要是内没有按法度办事的大臣和辅佐的人才，外没有敌对国家的忧患，往往容易亡国。所以说忧患使人生存，安逸享乐却使人败亡。

When Heaven is about to confer a great mission on a man, it first cultivates his mind by making him go through hardships and tribulations; makes his sinews and bones experience toil;

exposes his body to hunger; and inflicts him with poverty and knocks down everything he tries to build. By all these it stimulates his mind, hardens his original nature, and counteracts his weaknesses. People will always err, but it is only after making mistakes that they can correct themselves. Only when a man has been in a puzzle about things, not knowing what to do, can he rise in great vigor to reform himself. It will show in his face and be expressed in his words, so he will affect others. If in a state there is no ministers or advisors who handle affairs in accordance with moral standard, and outside the state there is no foreign aggression, the state will more often than not come to ruin. From these we can see how life springs from adversity and suffering, and ruin results from leading a life of easiness and pleasure.

求则得之，舍则失之，是求有益于得也，求在我者也。求之有道，得之有命，是求无益于得也，求在外者也。

（《孟子》尽心章句上）

【译文】

只要追求就能得到，放弃就会失去，这样的追求之所以一定有回报，是因为所追求的东西就在我自身。按正确的方法去追求，但是能否得到却到要看命运，这样的追求之所以不一定有回报，是因为所求的东西是身外之物。

Seek it, and you gain it. Abandon it, and you lose it. Seeking is conducive to getting, because the things sought for are those which are in ourselves. When the seeking for something is according to the proper means, yet the getting of it is dependent on fate, in that case, the seeking is not necessarily conducive to getting, because the things sought for are mere worldly possessions.

万物皆备于我矣。反身而诚，乐莫大焉。强恕而行，求仁莫近焉。

（《孟子》尽心章句上）

【译文】

万物的必然规律都存在于我的本心之中。反躬自问，自己是忠实地本着这些原则去做的，还有比这更大的快乐吗？如果遇到勉强的事只要本着推己及人的同情心去做，就是达到仁德最近的道路。

The inexorable laws of all things are prepared within me. If I reflect on myself and find that I have acted faithfully in conformity with these principles, is there any greater joy than that? Even if I encounter things that are difficult to manage, if I extend my own feelings to others, it will be the most direct approach to benevolence.

行之而不着焉，习矣而不察焉，终身由之而不知其道者，众也。

（《孟子》尽心章句上）

【译文】

做一件事却不明白为什么要做，习惯了就不想为什么会习惯，一辈子随波逐流不知道应该去何方，这样的人太多了。

Acting without understanding why to do so; practicing habitually without examining why the practice has become a common usage; drifting with the current all their life; this is the way of multitudes.

人不可以无耻。无耻之耻，无耻矣。

（《孟子》尽心章句上）

【译文】

人不可以不知道羞耻。对自己缺乏羞耻感感到羞耻，就可以免于羞耻了。

A man may not be without the sense of shame. When one is ashamed of lacking the sense of shame, he will afterwards not have occasion to be ashamed.

耻之于人大矣。为机变之巧者，无所用耻焉。不耻不若人，何若人有？

（《孟子》尽心章句上）

【译文】

羞耻心对于人来说关系重大。搞阴谋诡计的人是不知羞耻的。不以自己不如别人为羞耻，怎么赶得上别人呢？

The sense of shame is to a man of great importance. Those who engage in intrigues and conspiracy don't know what shame is. When one is not ashamed of not being as good as others, how can he catch up with others?

孟子谓宋勾践曰："子好游乎？吾语子游：人知之，亦嚣嚣；人不知，亦嚣嚣。"

曰："何如斯可以嚣嚣矣？"

曰："尊德乐义，则可以嚣嚣矣。故士穷不失义，达不离道。穷不失义，故士得己焉；达不离道，故民不失望焉。古之人，得志，泽加于民；不得志，修身见于世。穷则独善其身，达则兼善天下。"

（《孟子》尽心章句上）

【译文】

孟子对宋勾践说："你喜欢游说各国的君王吗？我告诉你游说的态度：别人理解也安详自得；别人不理解也安详自得。"

宋勾践问："怎样才能做到安详自得呢？"

孟子说："尊崇道德，满足于行正义，就可以安详自得了。所以有学识的人穷困时不会偏离正义，显达时不会背离道德。穷困时不偏离正义，所以不会失去自我；显达时不背离道德，所以百姓不会失望。古代的人，得志时把恩惠施于百姓；不得志时修养自身，以此表现于世人。穷困时让自己提高道德，显达时让天下人都提高道德。"

Mencius said to Song Gou Jian, "Are you fond of lobbying sovereigns? I will tell you about such lobbying. If a sovereign follows your counsels, take your ease and behave with composure. If he doesn't do so, be the same."

Song Gou Jian said, "What is to be done to secure this composure?"

Mencius answered, "Honor virtue and delight in uprightness, and so you may always be perfectly composed. Therefore, a learned person, though poverty – stricken, does not depart from uprightness; though prosperous, he does not deviate from the true path. Poverty – stricken and not departing from uprightness, so he won't lose his self. Prosperous and not deviating from the true path; so that the expectations of the people from him are not disappointed. When the men of antiquity realized their wishes, they conferred benefits on the people. If they were unable to realize their wishes, they cultivated their moral character, and demonstrated fine qualities to common people. If poor, they developed their own virtue; if prosperous, they made the people virtuous as well."

舜之居深山之中，与木石居，与鹿豕游，其所以异于深山之野人者几希。及其闻一善言，见一善行，若决江河，沛然莫之能御也。

（《孟子》尽心章句上）

【译文】

舜住在深山之中，家中只有树和石头，出门只见到鹿和野猪，和深山中一般人不同的地方很少。可是只要他听到好的话，看到好的行为，就像江河决口，一发而不可收，没有人能阻止得住。

When Shun was living in remote mountains, dwelling with the trees and rocks, and wandering among the deer and boars, the difference between him and the rude inhabitants of those remote mountains appeared very small. But when he heard good words, or saw a good deed, he was like a stream or a river bursting its banks, and flowing out in an irresistible flood.

无为其所不为，无欲其所不欲，如此而已矣。

（《孟子》尽心章句上）

【译文】

不干不该干的事，不想要不该要的物，这样就行了。

Don't do what shouldn't be done, and don't desire what shouldn't be desired. That's all there is to it.

人之有德慧术知者，恒存乎疢疾。独孤臣孽子，其操心也危，其虑患也深，故达。

（《孟子》尽心章句上）

【译文】

人的品德、智慧、本领、知识，往往产生于灾患之中。那些受疏远的大臣和妾所生的儿子，经常操心着危难之事，深深忧虑着祸患降临，所以能通达事理。

When people have virtue, intelligence, ability, and knowledge, it is usually because they have spent a long time in troubles. There are the slighted ministers and concubines' sons, who constantly worry about danger and disaster, and take deep precautions against calamity. Hence, they become reasonable.

有事君人者，事是君则为容悦者也。有安社稷臣者，以安社稷为悦者也。有天民者，达可行于天下而后行之者也。有大人者，正己而物正者也。

（《孟子》尽心章句上）

【译文】

有侍奉君王的人，那是用阿谀逢迎来使这个君王快乐的人；有安定国家的大臣，那是以安定国家为快乐的人。有顺应天命的无官位的人，那是等到他的做法能在天下行得通了再实行它的人。有圣人，那是先端正自己而外物随着端正的人。

There are persons who serve the sovereign, that is, they try to make the sovereign happy with their flatteries. There are ministers who seek the tranquility of the state, that is, they find their pleasure in securing that tranquility. There are the common people who comply with the mandate of Heaven, that is, they wait for the opportunity when their principles are practicable and then proceed to carry them out. There are sages, that is, they rectify themselves and others are rectified.

君子有三乐，而王天下不与存焉。父母俱存，兄弟无故，一乐也。仰不愧于天，俯不怍于人，二乐也。得天下英才而教育之，三乐也。

（《孟子》尽心章句上）

【译文】

有道德的人有三大快乐，而使天下归服不在其中。父母健在，兄弟平安，这是第一大快乐；上不愧对于天，下不愧对于人，这是第二大快乐；发现天下优秀的人才进行教育，这是第三大快乐。

A perfect gentleman has three things in which he delights, and making the people under Heaven yield is not one of them. That his father and mother are both alive, and his brothers are safe and sound; this is his first delight. That, when looking up, he has nothing to be ashamed of before Heaven, and, below, he has no guilty conscience before men; this is his second delight. That he can get from the land under Heaven the most talented individuals, and teach and nourish them; this is his third delight.

孔子登东山而小鲁，登泰山而小天下。故观于海者难为水，游于圣人之门者难为言。观水有术，必观其澜。日月有明，容光必照焉。流水之为物也，不盈科不行；君子之志于道也，不成章不达。

（《孟子》尽心章句上）

【译文】

孔子登上东山，就觉得鲁国变小了；登上泰山，就觉得整个天下都变小了。所以，观看过大海的人，便难以被其他的水所吸引；跟随圣人学习过的人，便难以被其他的言论所吸引。观看水有一定的方法，一定要看它的源泉。太阳、月亮照耀，要知道它们的光有源泉；流水有规律，不把坑坑洼洼填满不向前流；有道德的人立志掌握道，不积累一定的程度不能融会贯通。

Confucius ascended the eastern hill, and Lu appeared to

him small. He ascended the mount Tai, and all beneath the Heaven appeared to him small. So he who has watched the sea, finds it difficult to think anything of other waters; and he who has studied from the sage, finds it difficult to think anything of the words of others. There is an art in the contemplation of water. It is necessary to look at its source. The sun and moon shines brilliantly, because their light has its source. Flowing water is a thing which does not proceed till it has filled up every pit in its course. The virtuous men set their mind on the true way, they can only achieve mastery through a comprehensive study and the accumulation of knowledge.

　　饥者甘食，渴者甘饮，是未得饮食之正也，饥渴害之也。岂惟口腹有饥渴之害？人心亦皆有害。人能无以饥渴之害为心害，则不及人不为忧矣。

（《孟子》尽心章句上）

【译文】

　　饥饿的人觉得任何食物都是美味的，干渴的人觉得任何饮料都是可口的。他们不能吃喝出饮料和食物应有的正常滋味，是由于饥饿和干渴的妨害。难道只有嘴和肚子受到饥饿和干渴的妨害吗？人的内心也同样会受妨害。一个人能够不让饥饿和干渴那类的妨害去妨害内心，那就不用担心自己不如别人了。

For the hungry any food is sweet, and for the thirsty any drink is tasty. But they do not get the right taste of the food and the drink. Since the hunger and thirst impairs their palate. And is it only the mouth and belly which are impaired by hunger and thirst? Men's minds are also impaired by them. If a man can prevent things like hunger and thirst from impairing his mind, he need not worry about not being equal to other men.

柳下惠不以三公易其介。

（《孟子》尽心章句上）

【译文】

柳下惠不因为有大官做就改变他判断是非的原则。

Liu Xia Hui would not for the highest offices of state have changed his principle of distinguishing between true and false.

有为者辟若掘井，掘井九轫而不及泉，犹为弃井也。

（《孟子》尽心章句上）

【译文】

做事情像挖井，尽管挖了六七丈深但不见水就停下来，是自己废弃了井。

Doing things is like digging a well. If you dig fifteen metres and stop without hitting water, you are just throwing away the well.

桃应问曰："舜为天子，皋陶为士，瞽瞍杀人，则如之何？"孟子曰："执之而已矣。""然则舜不禁与？"

曰："夫舜恶得而禁之？夫有所受之也。"

"然则舜如之何？"

曰："舜视弃天下，犹弃敝蹤也。窃负而逃，遵海滨而处，终身欣然，乐而忘天下。"

（《孟子》尽心章句上）

【译文】

桃应问："舜是天子，皋陶是法官，假如舜的父亲瞽瞍杀了人，皋陶应该怎么办？"

孟子说："当然是把他逮捕了。"

桃应问："难道舜不阻止吗？"

孟子说："舜怎么会阻止呢？皋陶是按义理办事。"

桃应问："那舜该怎么办呢？"孟子说："舜把抛弃天子之位看得像抛弃破草鞋一样。他偷偷地背起父亲逃走，沿着海滨住下来，终身逍遥，乐得把曾经做过天子的事情忘掉。"

Tao Ying asked, "Shun being sovereign, and Gao Tao chief judge, if Shun's father, Gu Sou, had murdered a man, what would Gao Tao have done?"

Mencius said, "Gao Tao would simply have arrested him."

"But would not Shun have stopped such a thing?"

"How could Shun have stopped it? Gao Tao acted in accordance with what was upright."

"In that case what would Shun have done?"

"Shun would have regarded throwing away the throne as throwing away a worn-out straw sandal. He would stealthily have taken his father on his back and run away, and retired into solitude, living somewhere along the seashore. There he would have been happy to forget that he had once been the emperor."

食而弗爱，豕交之也；爱而不敬，兽畜之也。恭敬者，币之未将者也。恭敬而无实，君子不可虚拘。

（《孟子》尽心章句上）

【译文】

只是养活而不爱，那就像养猪一样；只是爱而不尊重，那就像养宠物一样。尊重之心应该是在赠给贤者币帛之前就有的。不是真正的尊重，有道德的人不会苟且留下。

To feed someone and not love him is the same as raising pigs. To love someone but not respect him is like keeping pets. Respect should come before the presentation of gifts. If respect is not genuine, a virtuous man will not accept the gift.

形色，天性也；惟圣人，然后可以践形。

（《孟子》尽心章句上）

【译文】

人的形体容貌是天赋予的，只有圣人才能把人的本性通过形体和容貌体现出来。

Although the bodily feature and looks of human are conferred by Heaven, only the sage can give expression to human nature through them.

天下有道，以道殉身；天下无道，以身殉道。未闻以道殉乎人者也。

（《孟子》尽心章句上）

修身 On Self-cultivation

【译文】

天下政治清明的时候，就让道义伴随自己的行为；天下政治黑暗的时候，就用修身的方法陪伴道义。只是没有听说过牺牲道义而屈从于他人的。

When right principles prevail throughout the state, one should enable moral principle to make a companion of his actions. When right principles disappear from the state, one should enable himself to make a companion of moral principle by cultivating his self. I have not heard of case that one sacrifices moral principle to submit to others.

于不可已而已者，无所不已；于所厚者薄，无所不薄也。其进锐者，其退速。

（《孟子》尽心章句上）

【译文】

不可以停止的工作都停止了，那就没有什么不可以停止的。该尊重的人都不尊重，那就没有什么人不可以薄待了。急于求成的人，后退也会快。

He, who stops the work that ought not to be stopped, will

think there is no work he can't stop. He, who doesn't respect people that ought to be respected, will think there is no one he can't slight. Those who rush for quick results will retreat before long.

君子之于物也，爱之而弗仁；于民也，仁之而弗亲。亲亲而仁民，仁民而爱物。

（《孟子》尽心章句上）

【译文】

有道德的人对于万物，有节制地取用，但谈不上用仁爱对待它们。对于百姓，用仁爱对待他们，但谈不上亲爱。亲爱亲人而仁爱百姓，仁爱百姓而爱惜万物。

The virtuous man treasures all things on earth but does not love them. He loves people, but is not affectionate to them. He is affectionate to his parents, and loves people. He loves people, and treasures creatures.

知者无不知也，当务之为急；仁者无不爱也，急亲贤之为务。

（《孟子》尽心章句上）

【译文】

智者没有什么事物不该知道，但是首先要知道当前最重要的事情；仁者没有什么人不该爱，但是首先要爱德才兼备的人。

There is nothing the wise should not understand，but they will first focus on the important things. There is no one the benevolent should not love，but they will first focus on the virtuous and able.

仁者以其所爱及其所不爱，不仁者以其所不爱及其所爱。

(《孟子》尽心章句下)

【译文】

仁者把对他喜爱的人的恩惠推及到他不喜欢的人，不仁者把对他不喜欢的人的祸害推及到他喜爱的人。

The benevolent men extend their kindness toward the people they like to those they dislike. Those who are the opposite of benevolent extend their injuries to the people they dislike to those they like.

三 修 身 On Self-cultivation

身不行道，不行于妻子；使人不以道，不能行于妻子。

（《孟子》尽心章句下）

【译文】

一个人自己不走正道，他的做法就是在妻子和孩子身上也行不通；不以正确的方法指使人，就是妻子和孩子也指使不了。

If a man does not walk in the right path, his way of doing things won't work even with his wife and children. If a man orders others not according to what is right, he won't be able to get the obedience of even his wife and children.

好名之人，能让千乘之国；苟非其人，箪食豆羹见于色。

（《孟子》尽心章句下）

【译文】

喜欢好名声的人能辞让有一千辆兵车的国家；但如果不真是能看轻富贵的人，一筐饭、一碗汤的得失也会让他变颜变色。

A man who loves fame may be able to decline a state of a thousand chariots; but if he is not really the man to do such a thing, the anxiety about the gain and loss of a basket of rice, or a bowl of soup, will appear in his countenance.

浩生不害问曰："乐正子，何人也？"孟子曰："善人也，信人也。""何谓善？何谓信？"

曰："可欲之谓善，有诸己之谓信。充实之谓美，充实而有光辉之谓大，大而化之之谓圣，圣而不可知之之谓神。乐正子，二之中，四之下也。"

（《孟子》尽心章句下）

【译文】

浩生不害问："乐正子是怎样的人？"孟子说："是好人，可信的人。""什么是好？什么是可信？"

孟子说："值得交往叫做好，真实地行善叫做可信；做善事非常多叫做美；做善事非常多、影响广泛叫大；"大"而且能广泛地教育人叫做圣；"圣"到了高深莫测的境界叫做神。乐正子，介于前两者之间，在后四者之下。"

Hao Sheng Bu Hai asked Mencius, "What sort of man is Yue Zheng Zi?" Mencius replied, "He is a good man, a sincere man." "What do you mean by 'good' and 'sincere'?"

Mencius said, "A man who is worth associating with is good. A man who carries out good works by actual efforts is sincere. He whose goodness has been filled up is what is called beautiful. He whose goodness has been filled up and his good influence is widespread is what is called great. Being great, a man also nourish the people to be benevolent, he is what is called a sage. When the sage is too high and deep to be measured, he is what is called a spirit – man. Yue Zheng Zi is between the first two characters, and below the last four. "

尧舜，性者也；汤武，反之也。动容周旋中礼者，盛德之至也；哭死而哀，非为生者也；经德不回，非以干禄也；言语必信，非以正行也。君子行法，以俟命而已矣。

（《孟子》尽心章句下）

【译文】

尧和舜有道德是出于本性；汤和武有道德是因为修身回复本性。行动容貌既自然又完全合乎礼，是最高的美德。哀悼死者应该出于真心悲痛，而不是为了给活着的人看；时刻依照道德做事，毫不动摇，这样做不是为了官职俸禄；说话务求合乎道德，并非借以显示自己的品行端正。有道德的人按必然的法则行事，把其他的交给命运。

Yao and Shun were virtuous by nature; Tang and Wu were so by returning to nature through self – cultivation. When your every action and expression operates perfectly in accordance with the rules of etiquette, that shows the extreme degree of virtue. Weeping for the dead should be from real sorrow, and not because of the living. Constantly acting in accordance with virtue without any bend, and from no view to post and salary. Speaking in conformity to virtue, not with any desire to do what is right. The virtuous man acts according to the inexorable law, and leaves the rest to fate.

　　说大人，则藐之，勿视其巍巍然。堂高数仞，榱题数尺，我得志弗为也；食前方丈，侍妾数百人，我得志弗为也；般乐饮酒，驱骋田猎，后车千乘，我得志弗为也。在彼者，皆我所不为也；在我者，皆古之制也，吾何畏彼哉？

（《孟子》尽心章句下）

【译文】

　　劝说地位高的人，要轻视他的地位，不要把他的显赫地位和权势放在眼里。哪怕他殿堂高两三丈，屋檐好几尺宽；如果我得志，并不屑于有这些。哪怕他佳肴摆成一片，侍奉的姬妾好几百；如果我得志，并不屑于有这些。哪怕他饮酒作乐，驰骋打猎，随从的车辆上千；如果我得志，并不屑于有这些。他所拥有的，都是我所不屑于有的；我所拥有的，是古代圣贤的法则。我为什么要怕他呢？

When persuading high officials it is necessary to take their position lightly, and not to look at their eminent position and power. Halls five or six metres high, with eaves one or two metres broad. If my wishes were to be realized, I would not have these. Delicacies are spread over two metres square, and female attendants and concubines are counted in the hundreds. If my wishes were to be realized, I would not have these. They enjoy themselves drinking, and go hunting, with hundreds of chariots following behind. If my wishes were to be realized, I would not have these. What they have are what I feel beneath my dignity to have; what I have are the principles of the ancients sages and men of virtue. Why should I stand in awe of them?

养心莫善于寡欲。其为人也寡欲，虽有不存焉者，寡矣；其为人也多欲，虽有存焉者，寡矣。

（《孟子》尽心章句下）

【译文】

修养内心最好的办法是减少欲望。一个人如果欲望很少，即使本性有所失去，那也是很少的；一个人如果欲望很多，即使本性还有所保留，那也是很少的。

To nourish the heart – mind there is nothing better than to limit the desires. If one has few desires, even if he may not be able to keep his original heart – mind in some things, they will be few. If one has many desires, even if he is able to keep his o-riginal heart – mind in some things, they will be few.

万章问曰："孔子在陈曰：'盍归乎来！吾党之士狂简，进取，不忘其初。'孔子在陈，何思鲁之狂士？"

孟子曰："孔子'不得中道而与之，必也狂狷乎！狂者进取，狷者有所不为也'。孔子岂不欲中道哉？不可必得，故思其次也。"

"敢问何如斯可谓狂矣？"曰："如琴张、曾皙、牧皮者，孔子之所谓狂矣。"

"何以谓之狂也？"曰："其志嘐嘐然，曰'古之人，古之人'。夷考其行而不掩焉者也。狂者又不可得，欲得不屑不洁之士而与之，是狷也，是又其次也。

"孔子曰：'过我门而不入我室，我不憾焉者，其惟乡原乎！乡原，德之贼也。'"曰："何如斯可谓之乡原矣？"

曰："'何以是嘐嘐也？言不顾行，行不顾言，则曰：古之人，古之人。行何为踽踽凉凉？生斯世也，为斯世也，善斯可矣。'阉然媚于世也者，是乡原也。"

万章曰："一乡皆称原人焉，无所往而不为原人，孔子以为德之贼，何哉？"

曰："非之无举也，刺之无刺也；同乎流俗，合乎污世；居之似忠信，行之似廉洁；众皆悦之，自以为是，而不可与入尧舜之道，故曰德之贼也。孔子曰：'恶似而非者：恶莠，恐其乱苗也；恶佞，恐其乱义也；恶利口，恐其乱信也；恶郑声，恐其乱乐也；恶紫，恐其乱朱也；恶乡原，恐其乱德也。'君子反经而已矣。经正，则庶民兴；庶民兴，斯无邪慝矣。"

（《孟子》尽心章句下）

【译文】

万章问："孔子在陈国说：'为什么不回去呢！我的那些学生们很狂放，追求很高，一直都是那样。'孔子在陈国，为什么思念鲁国的那些狂放之士呢？"

孟子说："孔子说，'不能和奉行中庸之道的人交往，就只能和志大才疏的人和洁身自好的人交往了。志大才疏的人勇于进取，洁身自好的人是不会干坏事的。'孔子难道不想和言行合于中庸之道的人交往吗？不能够得到，所以只能求次一等的罢了。"

万章问："请问什么样的人可以叫做志大才疏的人？"

孟子说："像琴张、曾皙、牧皮这些人，就是孔子所说的志大才疏的人。"

万章问："为什么说他们是志大才疏的人呢？"孟子说："他们志向很远大，口气也大，动不动就说'古人这样，古人那样。'可是考察他们的行为，却和说的话不相符。这种志大才疏的人如果也得不到，那就和洁身自好的人交往。这种谨慎的人，是比志大才疏的人次一等的人。孔子说：'从我家门口经过却不进我的屋里来，而我并不遗憾的，只有好好先生吧！好好先生是损害道德的人。'"

万章问："什么样的人可以称为好好先生呢？"

孟子说："好好先生嘲笑狂者说：'何必这样志向高、口气大呢？说的话不一定能和行为相符，行为不一定能和说的话相符。每件事都说古人呀，古人呀也没有用。'又嘲笑谨慎的人说：'何必这样落落寡合、不和人亲近呢？人既然生在这个世界上，就做这个世界上的人好了。对所有人都好就行了。'隐藏自己的内心，以求悦于所有人，就是好好先生。"

万章说："一乡的人都说他是厚道的人，他到处的表现也像个厚道的人，孔子却认为他是损害道德的人。这是为什么呢？"

孟子说："说这种人有什么不对，也举不出例子来；指责这种人却又好像无可指责。他只是媚俗、同流合污。心中好像有忠信，行为好像很廉洁。人们都喜欢他，他也以为自己很不错，但他的所作所为却和尧舜所走的道路不同，所以说他是损害道德的人。孔子说：'厌恶那些似是而非的东西：厌恶像禾苗的草，怕它搞乱苗床；厌恶花言巧语，怕它搞乱正义；厌恶夸夸其谈，怕它妨碍言行一致；厌恶郑国的乐曲，怕它搞乱礼乐；厌恶杂色，怕它搞乱正色；厌恶好好先生，怕他搞乱道德。'做有道德的人只不过是遵循人的本性罢了。回归本性，百姓就会变善良；百姓变善良，就不会有好好先生了。"

Wan Zhang asked, "When Confucius was staying in Chen, he said, 'Perhaps I should return home. The scholars of my school are ardent. They chase high targets, and they do so consistently.' Why did Confucius, when he was in Chen, miss the ardent scholars of Lu?"

Mencius replied, 'Since Confucius couldn't meet man who pursued the Golden Mean of moral characters, with whom he might have communicated, he had to associate with the ardent who had good aims but unequal ability, and those who were overcautious. The ardent dared to explore, the overcautious would keep themselves from what is wrong.' Did Confucius not wish to get men whose words and deeds conformed to the Golden Mean? But he was unable to find such people, he had to think of the next class."

"May I ask what one must be like, such that one can be called 'ardent'?"

"Men like Qin Zhang, Zeng Xi and Mu Pi were those whom Confucius called "ardent'."

"Why did he call them 'ardent'?"

Mencius said, "They had lofty ideals and talked big, frequently saying, 'The ancients did this, the ancients did that.' But if one examines their conduct, they didn't correspond with their words. When he found that he couldn't get those who are ardent, he wanted to associate with scholars who disdained to do what is not pure. Those were the overcautious, a class next to the ardent. Confucius said: 'When someone passes by my gate and does not enter, the only occasion I don't regret it is when it is a yes-man. These yes-men are thieves of virtue.'"

"What sort of people were these, that he called 'yes-men'?"

Mencius replied, "They jest at the ardent: 'Why are you so grand? Words can't agree with actions and actions can't conform to words. What's the point to say: 'the ancients, the ancients'?' And jest at the overcautious: 'Why are you so aloof and cold? Born in this age, we should be of this age, trying not to offend anybody is sufficient.' Hiding their heart, flattering their contemporaries, these are the 'yes-men'"

Wan Zhang said, "The people of a whole village call they kind persons. In all their conduct everywhere they are so. Why did Confucius consider them 'thieves of virtue'?"

Mencius answered: "If you want to blame them for something, there is nothing you can point to. If you want to criticise them, there is nothing to criticise. They court favor of the public and play a part in vile actions of the age. They seem to have faithfulness and sincerity in their hearts, and they do seem disinterested. The multitude delight in them. And they think themselves right. But their path is diverse from the path of Yao and Shun. On this account they are called 'thieves of virtue.'"

"Confucius said, 'I hate those appear right, but are actually wrong. I hate weeds that resemble grain, out of fear that they will mess up seedbed. I hate fine rhetoric, out of fear that it will mess up uprightness. I hate indulgence in verbiage, out of fear that it will hinder matching word to deed. I hate the music of Zheng, out of fear that it will mess up true music. I hate variegated color, out of fear that it will mess up pure color. I hate the 'yes – men', out of fear that they will mess up virtue. To be a virtuous man is simply to follow man's original nature. By returning to man's original nature, the people will become benevolent. When they are benevolent, there will be no more 'yes – man'."

The Quotations by Mencius

仁义、忠信

On Benevolence, Uprightness,
Faithfulness, and Sincerity

　　滕文公问曰："滕，小国也。竭力以事大国，则不得免焉。如之何则可？"

　　孟子对曰："昔者大王居邠，狄人侵之。事之以皮币，不得免焉；事之以犬马，不得免焉；事之以珠玉，不得免焉。乃属其耆老而告之曰：'狄人之所欲者，吾土地也。吾闻之也：君子不以其所以养人者害人。二三子何患乎无君？我将去之。'去邠，踰梁山，邑于岐山之下居焉。邠人曰：'仁人也，不可失也。'从之者如归市。

　　"或曰：'世守也，非身之所能为也。效死勿去。'

　　"君请择于斯二者。"

　　　　　　　　　　　　　　　（《孟子》梁惠王章句下）

【译文】

　　滕文公问："滕国是一个小国，竭尽所能服侍大国，仍然难免于灾难。怎么办才好呢？"

　　孟子回答说："从前，周太王居住在邠地，狄人来侵犯。贡奉出虎、豹、麋、鹿的皮和丝绸，没有能制止住侵犯；贡奉出良犬和骏马，也不能制止住侵犯。贡奉出珠宝，还是不能制止住侵犯。周太王便召集当地的长老，对他们说，'狄人希望得到的，是我们的土地。我听说过，有道德的人不会为了占有土地这样本该养育百姓之物而使百姓受害。你们何必担心没有君主呢？我要离开这里。'于是离开邠地，翻过梁山，在岐山下建立城池居住下来。邠地的百姓说，'这是一位仁德的人，不能失去他。'追随他的人像赶集一样。

　　"也有人说：'土地是祖先留下的，应该世代守护，不是

自己可以做主舍弃的。宁肯死也不离开。'

　　"请大王选择这两条道路之一。"

The Duke Wen of Teng asked Mencius, "Teng is a small state. Though I do my utmost to serve those powerful states, we can't escape suffering from them. What shall I do?"

Mencius replied, "Formerly, when King Tai dwelt in Bin, the northern barbarians were constantly making intrusions. He served them with skins and silks, but it didn't stop the intrusions. He served them with dogs and fine horses, but it didn't stop the intrusions. He served them with pearls and gems, but it didn't stop the intrusions. So he assembled the local elders and said, "What the barbarians want is the land. I have heard this: a virtuous man does not seek to possess land, which should be used to nourish the people, with the detriment to the people. Why should you be troubled about having no prince? I will leave here." Hence, he left Bin, crossed the mount Liang, built a town at the foot of mount Qi, and dwelt there. The people of Bin said, "He is a benevolent man. We must not lose him." Those who followed him looked like crowds hastening to market.

"On the other hand, some say, 'The country is a thing to be kept from generation to generation. One individual can't make arbitrary decision to give it up. Let him be prepared to die for it.'

"I ask Your Royal Highness to make your election between these two courses. "

仁者如射，射者正己而后发。发而不中，不怨胜己者，反求诸己而已矣。

（《孟子》公孙丑章句上）

【译文】

行仁德的人好比赛箭的人一样：射箭的人先端正自己的姿态然后放箭；如果没射中，不埋怨那些胜过自己的人，反躬自问罢了。

The man who would be benevolent is like the archer. The archer adjusts himself and then shoots. If he misses, he does not blame those who surpass himself. He simply examines himself.

自暴者，不可与有言也；自弃者，不可与有为也。言非礼义，谓之自暴也；吾身不能居仁由义，谓之自弃也。仁，人之安宅也；义，人之正路也。旷安宅而弗居，舍正路而不由，哀哉！

（《孟子》离娄章句上）

【译文】

自己糟蹋自己的人，和他没有什么可说的；自己抛弃自己的人，和他没有什么可做的。说话不公正、无礼貌，叫做自己糟蹋自己。自认为不能居仁心、走正直的路，叫做自己抛弃自己。仁，是人最安泰的住宅；义，是人最正确的道路。把最安泰的住宅空置起来不住，把最正确的道路舍弃在一边不走，真是可悲啊！

To those who act violently to themselves, there is noting to say. With those who throw themselves away, there is noting to do. Speaking unjustly and behaving rudely is acting violently to themselves. To think himself being unable to dwell in benevolence or pursue the path of uprightness is throwing himself away. Benevolence is the safest dwelling place of man, and uprightness is his straightest path. Alas for them, who leave the safest dwelling place empty and do not reside in it, and who abandon the straightest path and do not pursue it.

居下位而不获于上，民不可得而治也。获于上有道：不信于友，弗获于上矣；信于友有道：事亲弗悦，弗信于友矣；悦亲有道：反身不诚，不悦于亲矣；诚身有道：不明乎善，不诚其身矣。是故诚者，天之道也；思诚者，人之道也。至诚而不动者，未之有也；不诚，未有能动者也。

（《孟子》离娄章句上）

【译文】

职位低的人如果得不到上级的信任，是不能把百姓治理

（四）仁义、忠信 On Benevolence, Uprightness, Faithfulness, and Sincerity

好的。要得到上级的信任有方法：先要得到朋友的信任，否则也就得不到上级的信任了。要得到朋友的信任有方法：先要得到亲人的信任，否则也就得不到朋友的信任了。使亲人对自己信任是有办法的：不是真心为善，亲人是不会信任自己的。使自己对本心真诚是有办法的：不明白什么是善就不能使自己对本心真诚。所以，真实无伪是上天的原则；追求对本心真诚是做人的原则。极端真诚而不能够使别人感动的，是没有过的；不真诚是不能感动别人的。

When those occupying inferior posts do not obtain the confidence of those in higher positions, they can't succeed in governing the people. There is a way to obtain the confidence of those in higher positions. If one is not trusted by his friends, he will not obtain the confidence of those in higher positions. There is a way of being trusted by one's friends. If one is not trusted by his family members, he will not obtain the confidence of his friends. There is a way of being trusted by one's family members. If one, turning inwards and examining himself, finds a want of the genuineness to be benevolent, he will not obtain the confidence of his family members. There is a way to attain this genuineness in one's heart - mind. If a man does not understand what benevolence is, he will not attain this genuineness in his heart - mind. Therefore, genuineness is the way of Heaven. To pursue genuineness to original heart - mind is the way of man. Never has there been one possessed of complete genuineness, who did not move others. Never has there been one who had not genuineness who was able to move others.

大人者，言不必信，行不必果，惟义所在。

（《孟子》离娄章句下）

【译文】

有道德的人说话不考虑话是否能实现，做事不考虑是否有结果，他只考虑是否符合义。

The true gentleman does not think beforehand of his words if they may be realized, nor of his actions if they may bear fruit; he simply speaks and does what is upright.

人之所以异于禽于兽者几希，庶民去之，君子存之。舜明于庶物，察于人伦，由仁义行，非行仁义也。

（《孟子》离娄章句下）

【译文】

使人和禽兽不同的特征很少，一般人抛弃它，有道德的人保存它。舜明白事物的规律，深知人和人之间的必然关系，他自然而然地履行着仁和义，而不是为行仁义而行仁义。

That whereby man differs from the lower beasts is but
small. The mass of people cast it away, while perfect gentlemen preserve it. Shun clearly understood the law of natural
things，and knew the inexorable relations between individuals.
He walked spontaneously along the path of benevolence and up-
rightness；he did not need to pursue benevolence and uprightness.

孟季子问公都子曰："何以谓义内也？"

曰："行吾敬，故谓之内也。"

"乡人长于伯兄一岁，则谁敬？"曰："敬兄。"

"酌则谁先？"曰："先酌乡人。"

"所敬在此，所长在彼，果在外，非由内也。"公都子不能
答，以告孟子。

孟子曰："敬叔父乎？敬弟乎？彼将曰'敬叔父'。曰：
'弟为尸，则谁敬？'彼将曰'敬弟'。子曰：'恶在其敬叔父
也？'彼将曰：'在位故也。'子亦曰：'在位故也。庸敬在兄，
斯须之敬在乡人。'"季子闻之曰："敬叔父则敬，敬弟则敬，
果在外，非由内也。"公都子曰："冬日则饮汤，夏日则饮水，
然则饮食亦在外也？"

（《孟子》告子章句上）

【译文】

孟季子问公都子说：“怎么说义存在于人的心中呢？”

公都子说：“尊敬是从我的内心发出的，所以说义存在于人的心中。”

“一个本乡人比你的哥哥年长一岁，你尊敬谁？”公都子说：“尊敬哥哥。”

“在一起喝酒，先给谁斟酒？”公都子说：“先给本乡人斟酒。”

“心里尊敬一个人，却给另一个人斟酒。所以义是外界决定的，不是从内心发出的。”公都子无法回答，就把这件事告诉孟子。

孟子说：“你可以问：‘尊敬叔父呢？还是尊敬弟弟呢？’他会说：‘尊敬叔父。’你再问：‘弟弟成为祭祀的代理人，那该尊敬谁呢？’他会说：‘尊敬弟弟。’那你就问：‘为什么不说尊敬叔父呢？’他会说：‘是因为弟弟在受尊敬的地位。’你就说：‘给本乡人斟酒也是因为他在受尊敬的地位。平时尊敬哥哥，临时的场合尊敬本乡人。’”

孟季子听了，说：“该尊敬叔父时就尊敬叔父，该尊敬弟弟时就尊敬弟弟，义毕竟是外界决定的，而不是出自内心的。”

公都子说：“冬天喝热水，夏天喝凉水，难道喝什么是外界决定的吗？”

The Meng Ji Zi asked Gong Du Zi, saying, "On what

四 仁义、忠信 On Benevolence, Uprightness, Faithfulness, and Sincerity

ground is it said that uprightness exists in man's mind?"

Gong Du Zi replied, "The feeling of respect is from the depth of my heart, so I say uprightness exists in man's mind."

"Suppose the case of a villager older than your elder brother by one year, to whom would you show the greater respect?" Gong Du Zi said, "To my brother."

"But for which of them would you first pour a cup of wine at a feast?" Gong Du Zi said, "For the villager."

Meng Ji Zi said, "Now your feeling of respect rests on one, but you first pour a cup of wine for the other at a feast. Hence, uprightness is determined by external factors, it is not from one's heart." Gong Du Zi was unable to find an answer, and told the conversation to Mencius.

Mencius said, "You should ask him, 'Which do you respect more, your uncle, or your younger brother?' He will answer, 'My uncle.' Ask him again, 'If your younger brother is personating the agent to offer sacrifices in a ceremony, to whom do you show the greater respect?' He will say, 'To my younger brother.' Then you can say, 'But you said the respect is due to your uncle.' He will reply to this, 'Because my younger brother occupies the respectable position.' And you can say, 'I first pour a cup of wine for the villager at a feast, because he occupies the respectable position. So on ordinary occasions my respect is rendered to my elder brother; on special occasions it is rendered to the villager.'"

Meng Ji Zi heard this and said, "When respect is due to my uncle, I respect my uncle, and when respect is due to my younger brother, I respect my younger brother. Uprightness after all is determined by external factors, and does not proceed from heart."

Gong Du Zi said, "In winter we drink hot water, in summer we drink cold water. Could it be said that drinking is depended on what is external?"

仁，人心也；义，人路也。舍其路而弗由，放其心而不知求，哀哉！人有鸡犬放，则知求之；有放心，而不知求。学问之道无他，求其放心而已矣。

（《孟子》告子章句上）

【译文】

仁是人心最本质的特征；义是人应该走的道路。放弃了应该走的道路不走，丢失了最本质的特征却不知道寻求，真是悲哀啊！有的人鸡狗丢失了倒知道去找，本心丢失了却不知道去寻求。学问的关键不是别的，就是把那失去了的本心找回来罢了。

Benevolence is the essence of man's original heart – mind, and uprightness is the path man ought to follow. To abandon

the true path and not follow it, or to lose the essence of heart -
mind and not know enough to seek it, this is a pity indeed!
When men's chickens and dogs are lost, they know to seek for
them, but they lose their original heart - mind, and do not
know to seek for it. The kernel of learning is nothing else but
to seek for the lost mind.

仁之胜不仁也，犹水胜火。今之为仁者，犹以一杯水，救
一车薪之火也；不熄，则谓之水不胜火，此又与于不仁之甚者
也。亦终必亡而已矣。

（《孟子》告子章句上）

【译文】

仁能胜过不仁，就像水可以灭火一样。但现在奉行仁德
的人，就像用一杯水去灭一车柴草所燃烧的大火一样。灭不
了，就说水不能灭火。这样的说法正好又大大助长了那些不
仁之徒，结果连他们原本奉行的一点仁德也必然会最终
失去。

Benevolence subdues its opposite just as water subdues
fire. But nowadays those who practice benevolence do it as if
they try to put out a burning cartload of faggots with a cup of
water. And when the flames doesn't go out, they say that water can't put out fire. This way of saying encourages those who

are not benevolent. As a result they lose that small amount of benevolence they practice.

五谷者，种之美者也；苟为不熟，不如荑稗。夫仁亦在乎熟之而已矣。

（《孟子》告子章句上）

【译文】

　　五谷是庄稼中的好品种。但要是不成熟，还不如荑米和稗子。仁也在于它的成熟罢了。

Of all crops the five cereals are the best breeds, yet if they are not mature, they are not even as good as the tares. The value of benevolence depends on its being brought to maturity.

　　宋牼将之楚，孟子遇于石丘。曰："先生将何之？"

　　曰："吾闻秦楚构兵，我将见楚王说而罢之。楚王不悦，我将见秦王说而罢之，二王我将有所遇焉。"

　　曰："轲也请无问其详，愿闻其指。说之将何如？"

　　曰："我将言其不利也。"

　　曰："先生之志则大矣，先生之号则不可。先生以利说秦楚之王，秦楚之王悦于利，以罢三军之师，是三军之士乐罢而悦于利也。为人臣者怀利以事其君，为人子者怀利以事其父，为人弟者怀利以事其兄。是君臣、父子、兄弟终去仁义，怀利以相接，然而不亡者，未之有也。先生以仁义说秦楚之王，秦楚之王悦于仁义，而罢三军之师，是三军之士乐罢而悦于仁义也。为人臣者怀仁义以事其君，为人子者怀仁义以事其父，为人弟者怀仁义以事其兄，是君臣、父子、兄弟去利，怀仁义以相接也。然而不王者，未之有也。何必曰利?"

（《**孟子**》告子章句下）

【译文】

宋牼准备到楚国去，孟子在石丘这个地方遇上了他。孟子问："先生准备到哪里去?"

宋牼说："我听说秦楚两国交战，我准备去见楚王，劝说他罢兵。如果楚王不听，我准备去见秦王，劝说他罢兵。在两个国王中，我总会劝说通一个。"

孟子说："我不想问得太详细，只想知道你的大意，你准备怎样去劝说他们?"

宋牼说："我会告诉他们，交战对他们不利。"

孟子说："先生的动机非常好，可是先生的理由却不好。先生用利去劝说秦王和楚王，秦王和楚王因为趋利避害，停止军事行动；军队的官兵也因为对自己有利而乐于罢兵。做臣的怀着趋利避害的念头来侍奉君王，做儿子的怀着趋利避害的念头来侍奉父亲，做弟弟的怀着趋利避害的念头来侍奉哥哥。这就会使君臣之间、父子之间、兄弟之间最终完全失去仁义，怀着趋利避害的念头来互相对待。这样不使国家灭亡的，是没有的。先生要是用仁义的道理劝说秦王和楚王，让秦王和楚王因为喜好仁义，所以停止军事行动；军队的官兵也因为喜好仁义而乐于罢兵。做臣的心怀仁义来侍奉君王，做儿子的心怀仁义来侍奉父亲，做弟弟的心怀仁义来侍奉哥哥，这就会使君臣之间、父子之间、兄弟之间摆脱利害关系的考虑，心怀仁义来互相对待。这样还不能使天下归服的，是没有的。为什么要去谈'利'呢？"

Song Keng was on his way to Chu, Mencius met him in Shi Qiu. Mencius asked him, "Where are you going, sir?"

Song Keng replied, "I have heard that Qin and Chu are fighting together, and I am going to see the King of Chu and try to persuade him to cease hostilities. If he won't follow my advice, I shall go to see the King of Qin, and try to persuade him. I am sure I shall have success with one or other of the two Kings."

Mencius said, "I will not venture to ask about the details, but I would like to know the gist of your argument. How are you going to persuade them?"

Song Keng answered, "I will explain to them the war is unprofitable to them."

Mencius said, "Your intention is lofty indeed, but your slogan is wrong.

"If you, starting from the point of profit, offer your persuasive counsels to the Kings of Qin and Chu, and they call off their armies because they are drawn to profit; and the officers and men are pleased with cessation of hostilities because it is profitable to them. Then it means ministers will serve their sovereign in the pursuit of profit; sons will serve their fathers in the pursuit of profit; and younger brothers will serve their elder brothers in the pursuit of profit. The result will be that in their mutual relations, sovereign and subject, father and son, elder brother and younger brother, all cherish the profit motive to the total exclusion of benevolence and uprightness. There has never been such a state that follows this path without bringing destruction on itself. If you, starting from the ground of benevolence and uprightness, offer your counsels to the Kings of Qin and Chu, and they call off their armies because they were drawn to benevolence and uprightness; and the officers and men are pleased with cessation of hostilities because they find their pleasure in benevolence and uprightness. Then it means ministers will serve their sovereign, cherishing the principles of benevolence and uprightness; sons will serve their fathers, and younger brothers will serve their elder brothers, in the same way. The result will be that in their mutual relations, sovereign and subject, father and son, elder brother and younger brother, all cherish the principles of benevolence and uprightness, abandoning the thought of profit. There has never been such a state that follows this path without making the people under Heaven yield. What is the point of mentioning the word 'profit'?"

人之所不学而能者，其良能也；所不虑而知者，其良知也。孩提之童无不知爱其亲者，及其长也，无不知敬其兄也。亲亲，仁也；敬长，义也；无他，达之天下也。

（《孟子》尽心章句上）

【译文】

人不经学习就能做的，那是良能；不经思考就能知道的，那是良知。年幼的孩子，没有不知道要爱他们的父母的；长大后，没有不知道要敬重他们的兄长的。爱父母就是仁，敬兄长就是义，这没有别的原因，只因为仁和义是通行于天下的。

The ability possessed by men without having been acquired by learning is intuitive ability, and the knowledge possessed by them without the exercise of thought is their intuitive knowledge. Young children all know to love their parents, and when they are grown a little, they all know to love their elder brothers. Filial benevolence is the working of benevolence. Fraternal affection is the working of righteousness. There is no other reason for those feelings; they belong to all people under Heaven.

（四）仁义、忠信 On Benevolence, Uprightness, Faithfulness, and Sincerity

公孙丑曰："伊尹曰：'予不狎于不顺。'放太甲于桐，民大悦。太甲贤。又反之，民大悦。贤者之为人臣也，其君不贤，则固可放与？"

孟子曰："有伊尹之志，则可；无伊尹之志，则篡也。"

（《孟子》尽心章句上）

【译文】

公孙丑说："伊尹说：'我看不惯有背仁义的人。'他把太甲放逐到桐邑，百姓很高兴。太甲变好了。又恢复他的王位，百姓很高兴。贤者作为臣，他的君王不道德，可以放逐吗？"

孟子曰："有伊尹的志向，就可以；要是没有伊尹的志向，就是篡位。"

Gong Sun Chou said, "Yi Yin said, 'I can't be near and see those who act contrary to benevolence.' He exiled Tai Jia to Tong. The people were much pleased. When Tai Jia became virtuous, he restored his throne, and the people were again much pleased. When the virtuous are ministers, may they indeed exile their sovereigns in this way when they are not virtuous?"

Mencius replied, "If they have the same ideal as Yi Yin, they may. If they have not the same ideal, it would be usurpation."

王子垫问曰："士何事?"孟子曰："尚志。"曰："何谓尚志?"

曰："仁义而已矣。杀一无罪,非仁也;非其有而取之,非义也。居恶在? 仁是也;路恶在? 义是也。居仁由义,大人之事备矣。"

(《孟子》尽心章句上)

【译文】

齐王之子垫问:"闲居的学者干什么工作?"

孟子说:"使自己心志高尚。"

王子垫问:"什么叫使自己心志高尚?"

孟子说:"奉行仁和义罢了。杀死一个无罪的人,是不仁;不是自己的东西却去占有,是不义。立足于哪里? 立足于仁;走什么道路? 走正义的道路。立足于仁而走正义的道路,优秀人物干工作的条件就齐备了。"

The King's son, Dian, asked Mencius, "What is the business of the unemployed scholar?"

Mencius replied, "To elevate his ideal. "

Dian asked, "What do you mean by elevating the ideal?"

Mencius answered, "Pursuing benevolence and uprightness. Killing a single innocent man is not benevolent. Taking something which is not yours is not upright. Where should one dwell? In benevolence. What path should he pursue? Uprightness. When one base himself on benevolence, and travel through the path of uprightness, the preconditions for an outstanding person to complete his work are all ready."

不信仁贤，则国空虚。无礼义，则上下乱。无政事，则财用不足。

（《孟子》尽心章句下）

【译文】

不信任有道德、有能力的人，国家就会没有可用的人。不讲礼义，主次就会混乱。没有好的政治，国家的财物就会匮乏。

If men of virtue and ability are not trusted, a state will become empty. Without the observance of etiquette and uprightness, the incidental will be put before the fundamental. Without good politics, there will not be wealth sufficient for the expenditure.

仁也者，人也。合而言之，道也。

（《孟子》尽心章句下）

【译文】

仁就是做人的原则。仁和人合起来讲就是人生正道。

Benevolence is the characteristic of man. As embodied in man's conduct, it is called the right way of man.

人皆有所不忍，达之于其所忍，仁也；人皆有所不为，达之于其所为，义也。人能充无欲害人之心，而仁不可胜用也；人能充无穿窬之心，而义不可胜用也。人能充无受尔汝之实，无所往而不为义也。士未可以言而言，是以言餂之也；可以言而不言，是以不言餂之也，是皆穿窬之类也。

（《孟子》尽心章句下）

【译文】

人都有不忍心干的事，努力做好应该干的事，就是仁；人都有觉得理应不干的事，努力做好理应干的事，就是义。人能把不愿意害人的心加以发展，仁就用不完；人能把不肯偷盗的心加以发展，义就用不完；人能把不甘心背不义之名的心加以发展，做的事就没有不合乎义的。不可以同别人谈的却同他谈，是用话为自己牟利；可以同他谈的却不同他谈，是用沉默为自己牟利，这些都属于偷盗之类。

All men have some things which they can't bear to do. If one exerts himself to do what he can stand to do, the result will be benevolence. All men have some things which they deem they should not do. If one exerts himself to do what he deems he should do, the result will be uprightness. If a man can fully develop the heart which is unwilling to injure others, his benev-olence will be too much for use. If he can fully develop the heart which refuses to steal, his uprightness will be too much for use. If he can fully develop the heart for which the bad reputa-tion of being unjust is inconceivable, his acts will be able to conform to uprightness in all places and under any circum-stances. When a gentleman speaks what he ought not to speak, this is to seek benefits by speaking. When he does not speak what he ought to speak, this is to seek benefits by keeping si-lence. Both can be considered as thievery.

The Quotations by Mencius

王道、仁政

On Benevolent Government

孟子见梁惠王。王曰："叟不远千里而来，亦将有以利吾国乎？"

孟子对曰："王何必曰利？亦有仁义而已矣。王曰'何以利吾国'？大夫曰'何以利吾家'？士庶人曰'何以利吾身'？上下交征利而国危矣。万乘之国弑其君者，必千乘之家；千乘之国弑其君者，必百乘之家。万取千焉，千取百焉，不为不多矣。苟为后义而先利，不夺不餍。未有仁而遗其亲者也，未有义而后其君者也。王亦曰仁义而已矣，何必曰利？"

（《孟子》梁惠王章句上）

【译文】

孟子拜见梁惠王。梁惠王说："老先生不远千里而来，一定会对我的国家有很大的利益吧？"

孟子回答说："大王为什么提利益呢？只要讲仁和义就可以了。要是王说：'怎样对我的国家有利益？'大夫说：'怎样对我的家族有利益？'士和百姓说：'怎样对我有利益？'上下相互追逐利益，国家就危险了。在拥有一万辆兵车的国家里，杀掉国君的，一定是拥有一千辆兵车的大夫。在拥有一千辆兵车的国家里，杀掉国君的，一定是拥有一百辆兵车的大夫。在拥有一万辆兵车的国家里，大夫拥有一千辆兵车。在拥有一千辆兵车的国家里，大夫拥有一百辆兵车。这些大夫的产业不能不说是很多了。但是，要是把义抛开去追逐利益，那些大夫不把国君的产业夺去是永远不能满足的。从没有讲仁的人遗弃他的父母的，也没有讲义的人对他的君王怠慢的。大王只要讲仁和义就可以了。为什么要讲利益呢?"

Mencius went to see King Hui of Liang. The King said, "Venerable sir, you have come here without regarding hundreds of miles as very distant. You must surely have some ideas about how to benefit my state."

Mencius replied, "Why must Your Majesty emphasize the word 'benefit'? All that matters is that there should be benevolence and uprightness. If the King says, 'How can I benefit my state?' and the high officials say, "How can I benefit my clan?" and the gentlemen and common people say, "How can I benefit myself?" When those above and those below struggle against each other for benefit the state will be in danger. When the King of a state of ten thousand chariots is murdered, the murderer must be a high official with a thousand chariots. When the King of a state of a thousand chariots is murdered, the murderer must be a high official with a hundred chariots. Those with one thousand chariots in a state of ten thousand chariots, or one hundred in a state of a thousand, had quite a bit. But when benefit is put before what is upright, they are not satisfied without grabbing all. There has never been a benevolent person who neglected his parents or an upright person who slighted his lord. Let Your Majesty say, 'All I am concerned with is benevolence and uprightness.' What is the point of mentioning the word 'benefit'?"

梁惠王曰："寡人之于国也，尽心焉耳矣。河内凶，则移其民于河东，移其粟于河内。河东凶亦然。察邻国之政，无如寡人之用心者。邻国之民不加少，寡人之民不加多，何也?"

孟子对曰："王好战，请以战喻。填然鼓之，兵刃既接，弃甲曳兵而走。或百步而后止，或五十步而后止。以五十步笑百步，则何如?"

曰："不可，直不百步耳，是亦走也。"

曰："王如知此，则无望民之多于邻国也。不违农时，谷不可胜食也；数罟不入洿池，鱼鳖不可胜食也；斧斤以时入山林，材木不可胜用也。谷与鱼鳖不可胜食，材木不可胜用，是使民养生丧死无憾也。养生丧死无憾，王道之始也。

"五亩之宅，树之以桑，五十者可以衣帛矣；鸡豚狗彘之畜，无失其时，七十者可以食肉矣；百亩之田，勿夺其时，数口之家可以无饥矣；谨庠序之教，申之以孝悌之义，颁白者不负戴于道路矣。七十者衣帛食肉，黎民不饥不寒，然而不王者，未之有也。

"狗彘食人食而不知检，涂有饿莩而不知发；人死，则曰：'非我也，岁也。'是何异于刺人而杀之，曰：'非我也，兵也。'王无罪岁，斯天下之民至焉。"

（《孟子》梁惠王章句上）

【译文】

梁惠王说："我对于国家的事，真是费尽了心思。河内的地方遭灾，就把那里能迁移的百姓迁移到河东，把河东的部分粮食运到河内赈济不能迁移的百姓。如果河东遭了灾也是一样。考察邻国的政治，没有我这样用心的。可是离开邻国的百姓没有增加，到我国来的百姓也没有增加，这是为什么？"

孟子回答说："大王喜好打仗，那就拿打仗来做比方。战鼓隆隆，兵刃刚接触，两个士兵就丢下盔甲拖着兵器逃跑，有一个跑了一百步后停下来，有一个跑了五十步后停下来。你觉得那个跑了五十步的可以嘲笑跑了一百步的吗？"

梁惠王对孟子说："不可以。那个嘲笑别人的士兵，只不过逃跑了不到一百步，但实质上也是逃跑。"

孟子说："大王如果知道这层道理，就不会指望邻国的百姓来到自己的国家。不违背农时征用民力，粮食就吃不完；不把细密的鱼网撒入池塘，鱼鳖就吃不完；伐木砍柴的刀斧只在适当的时候进入山林，木材就用不尽。粮食、鱼鳖吃不完，木材用不尽，这样就能使百姓对养生和送死都没有不满的。百姓对养生和送死没有不满，这是仁政的开端。

"让每家有五亩大的宅院，种植上桑树，过了五十岁的人就可以穿上丝绵衣了，饲养鸡狗猪，按时繁殖，过了七十岁的人就可以有肉吃了。让每家有一百亩的耕地，按节气耕种，几口人的家庭就可以不挨饿了。认真办好学校的教育，反复讲父子之爱和兄弟之情，就不会有头发花白的老人身背、头顶物件走在路上了。过了七十岁的人有丝绵衣穿、有肉吃，年轻人也不会挨冻受饿。这样还不能被百姓拥戴的王，从来也没有过。

　　"可在这里富人的猪狗吃掉了百姓的粮食，却不知道检查、禁止。道路上有饿死的人却不知道发放赈济。人饿死了，就说：'这不是我的错，是年成不好。'这和用兵器杀了人，却说：'不是我杀的，是兵器杀的。'有什么两样？大王要是不再归罪于年成好坏，天下的百姓就会来归顺了。"

King Hui of Liang said, "I do exert my mind to the utmost in the government of my kingdom. When there is disaster in He Nei, I transport the removable people to He Dong and bring a part of the grain in He Dong to He Nei to relieve the victims. When there is disaster in He Dong, I do likewise. On examining the government of the neighboring states, I don't find that there is any ruler who exerts his mind as I do. Yet the people leaving the neighboring states do not increase, and the people coming to my kingdom do not increase. How is this?"

Mencius replied, "Your majesty is fond of war. Let me draw an analogy with war. The war drum is beating, the soldiers move forward. After the battle is engaged, the soldiers throw off their armors and flee, dragging their weapons behind them. One soldier runs a hundred paces and stops; another runs fifty paces and stops. What would you think if the one who ran fifty paces were to laugh at the one who ran a hundred paces?"

The Kind said, "He should not do so. Though he didn't run a hundred paces, he still ran away."

Mencius said, "If Your Majesty knows this, you shouldn't expect people to move to your state from the neighboring states. If the seasons of husbandry be not interfered with, the grain will be more than can be eaten. If close nets are not allowed to enter the ponds, the fishes and turtles will be more than can be consumed. If the axes and bills only enter the mountain forest in due season, the wood will be more than can be used. When the grain and fish and turtles are more than can be eaten, and there is more wood than can be used, this enables the people to nourish their living and mourn for their dead without resentment. Nourishing the living and mourning the dead without resentment is the beginning of benevolent government.

"Let each household has a messuage of an acre, where mulberry trees can be planted, and persons of fifty years may be clothed with silk floss. In keeping fowls, dogs, and pigs, let not their times of breeding be neglected, and persons of seventy years may eat flesh. Let each household has the farmland of twenty acres. If the seasons of husbandry be not interfered with, the family of several mouths that is supported by it shall not suffer from hunger. Pay careful attention to education in schools, instilling filial benevolence and fraternal affection into the mind of the young, and grey – haired men will not be on the roads, carrying burdens on their backs or on their heads. There has never been a case where the people of seventy were wearing silk floss and eating flesh and the black – haired people were free from cold and hunger, where the King didn't enjoy the love and esteem of his subjects.

"But in your kingdom dogs and pigs eat the food of men, and you don't control it. There are bodies of people died from starvation on the roads, and it doesn't occur to you to provide aid. When people die from starvation, you say, 'It's not my fault; it is owing to the year.' How is this different from stabbing a man and killing him and saying, 'it wasn't me; it was the weapon'? If Your Majesty ceases to put the blame on the year, the people under Heaven will come to you."

庖有肥肉，厩有肥马，民有饥色，野有饿莩，此率兽而食人也。兽相食，且人恶之。为民父母，行政不免于率兽而食人。恶在其为民父母也？仲尼曰："始作俑者，其无后乎！"为其象人而用之也。如之何其使斯民饥而死也？

（《孟子》梁惠王章句上）

【译文】

厨房里有肥嫩的肉，马厩里养着健壮的马，可是百姓们面带饥色，野外躺着饿死的人。这等于是率领着野兽吃人。野兽自相残杀，人尚且厌恶它们。作为百姓的父母官，施行政治却不免于率领野兽吃人。这怎么是百姓的父母官呢？孔子说："最早制作人形偶像陪葬的人，该断绝后代。"这是因为用像人的东西来陪葬。何况让老百姓活活地饿死呢？

In your kitchen there are loads of meat; in your stables there are healthy horses. But your people have the look of hunger, and on the wilds there are bodies of people died from starvation. This is equivalent to leading on beasts to devour men. Beasts feed on each other, and men despise them for doing so. Being the parent of his people, you administers your government so as to be chargeable with leading on beasts to devour men, where is your parental relation to the people?

Confucius said "Was he not without posterity who first made images of man to bury with the dead?" Because that man made the likeness of men to bury with the dead. Let alone to cause the people to die of hunger?

地方百里而可以王。王如施仁政于民，省刑罚，薄税敛，深耕易耨。壮者以暇日修其孝悌忠信，入以事其父兄，出以事其长上，可使制梃以挞秦楚之坚甲利兵矣。彼夺其民时，使不得耕耨以养其父母，父母冻饿，兄弟妻子离散。彼陷溺其民，王往而征之，夫谁与王敌？故曰："仁者无敌。"

（《孟子》梁惠王章句上）

【译文】

只要有一百里的土地就可以使天下归服。大王如果对百姓施行仁政，减免刑罚，减轻赋税，使百姓能深耕细作，及时除草。让身强力壮的人有时间修养父子之爱、兄弟之情，和尽责、诚实的品德。在家侍奉父母兄长，出门尊敬长辈上级。这样就算让他们制作木棒也可以打击有坚实铠甲和锋利兵器的秦楚军队了。因为秦国、楚国的统治者剥夺了百姓的生产时间，使他们不能靠耕种来赡养父母。父母挨冻受饿，兄弟妻子离散。他们使百姓深陷在苦难中，大王去征伐他们，百姓有谁会和大王为敌呢？所以说："仁德的人是无敌于天下的。"

With a territory which is only thirty miles square, it is possible to make the people under Heaven yield. If Your Majesty will put in practice a benevolent government, being mitigating the punishments, and reducing the taxes, so causing that the fields shall be ploughed deep, and the weeding of them be in time, and that the strong - bodied shall have time to cultivate

their filial benevolence and fraternal affection, and the fine
qualities of faithfulness and sincerity. So that they can serve
their fathers and elder brothers when they are at home, and
their elders and superiors when they are out in the world.
These people will be able, with sticks, to give a beating to the
troops of Qin and Chu with their solid armours and sharp weapons. For the rulers of those states rob their people of their
time, so that they can't plough and weed their fields in order to
support their parents. Their parents suffer from cold and hunger. Their brothers, wives, and children are separated and
scattered about. Those rulers bring deep misery to their people. If Your Majesty go to correct them, who will oppose Your
Majesty? So people say, "The benevolent is ever–victorious."

　　孟子见梁襄王。出，语人曰："望之不似人君，就之而不
见所畏焉。卒然问曰：'天下恶乎定?'吾对曰：'定于一。'
'孰能一之?'对曰：'不嗜杀人者能一之。''孰能与之?'对
曰：'天下莫不与也。王知夫苗乎? 七八月之间旱，则苗槁矣。
天油然作云，沛然下雨，则苗浡然兴之矣。其如是，孰能御
之? 今夫天下之人牧，未有不嗜杀人者也，如有不嗜杀人者，
则天下之民皆引领而望之矣。诚如是也，民归之，由水之就
下，沛然谁能御之?'"

（《孟子》梁惠王章句上）

【译文】

　　孟子拜见梁襄王。出来后，告诉人说："远看他不像国君，走近他也看不出让人敬畏的地方。他急着问我：'天下怎样才能安定？'

　　"我回答说：'统一才会安定。'

　　"他问：'哪一个国君能统一天下？'

　　"我回答：'不喜欢杀人的国君能统一天下。'

　　"他又问：'谁会归服他呢？'

　　"我回答：'天下没有不愿意归服他的人。大王知道禾苗的情况吗？在五、六月间天旱的时候，禾苗就干枯了。如果天上乌云密布，下起大雨来，禾苗便会蓬勃生长起来。这样的情况，谁能阻挡得住呢？现在天下的国君们，没有一个不喜欢杀人的。如果有一个不喜欢杀人的国君，那么，天下的百姓都会伸长脖子期待着他来解救的。真是这样，百姓归服他，就会像水向下流一样，浩浩荡荡谁能阻挡得住呢？'"

Mencius went to see the King Xiang of Liang.

When he came out, he said to some people, "When I looked at him from a distance, he did not appear like a sovereign; when I got closer, I saw nothing venerable about him. He asked me eagerly, 'How can the land under Heaven be settled?' I replied, 'It can be settled through unity.'

"He asked, 'Who can unify it?'

"I replied, 'He who doesn't like killing people can unify it.'

"He asked, 'Who will yield to him?'

"I replied, 'There is no one under Heaven who would not yield to him. Do Your Majesty understand the way of the growing grain? If there is a drought in the fifth or sixth months, the plants wither. But if dark clouds gather in the sky, and it rains heavily, the grain will come to life and grow with vigor. When it does so, who can stop it? Now among the Kings under Heaven, there is not one who doesn't like killing people. If there were one who didn't like killing people, all the people under Heaven would raise their head and look forward to being saved by him. In this case, the people would yield to him, as water flows downwards like a great flood, who can stop it?"

老吾老，以及人之老；幼吾幼，以及人之幼。天下可运于掌。诗云：'刑于寡妻，至于兄弟，以御于家邦。'言举斯心加诸彼而已。故推恩足以保四海，不推恩无以保妻子。古之人所以大过人者无他焉，善推其所为而已矣。

（《孟子》梁惠王章句上）

【译文】

尊敬我的长辈，从而推广到尊敬别人的长辈。爱护我的儿女，从而推广到爱护别人的儿女。这样，要想让天下归服就像在手中转动小物件那样容易了。《诗经》上说，"先给妻子做榜样，再推广到兄弟。再推广到封地和国家。"这就是说把这样的好心扩大到其他所有人就行了。所以，由近及远地把恩惠推广开，就足以安定天下。不这样，甚至连自己的妻子和儿女都保护不了。古代的圣贤之所以远远超过一般人，没有别的诀窍，只因他们善于推广他们的好行为罢了。

Treat your elders with reverence, and extend it to the elders of others; treat your young ones with kindness, and extend it to the young ones of others. On doing this, to make all the people under Heaven yield to you is as easy as making a small thing go round in your palm. It's said in the Book of Poetry, "First set a good example to his wife. Then extend it to his brothers. And in this way he controlled his clan and the state." This means that all you need to do is just extending your kindly heart to all others. So, if one extends his kindness, he can settle the land under Heaven; if he doesn't do so, he won't even be able to protect his wife and children. The way in which the ancient sages and men of virtue have greatly exceeded the common people is none other than this: they were simply good at extending their kindness.

无恒产而有恒心者，惟士为能。若民，则无恒产，因无恒心。苟无恒心，放辟，邪侈，无不为已。及陷于罪，然后从而刑之，是罔民也。焉有仁人在位，罔民而可为也？是故明君制民之产，必使仰足以事父母，俯足以畜妻子，乐岁终身饱，凶年免于死亡。然后驱而之善，故民之从之也轻。今也制民之产，仰不足以事父母，俯不足以畜妻子，乐岁终身苦，凶年不免于死亡。此惟救死而恐不赡，奚暇治礼义哉？

（《孟子》梁惠王章句上）

【译文】

没有稳定的产业收入却有稳定的本心，只有受过教育的人才能做到，至于一般人，如果没有稳定的产业收入，本心就不会稳定。本心一旦不稳定，就可能胡作非为，什么事都做得出来。等到他们犯了罪，然后才去加以处罚，这等于是陷害他们。哪里有仁慈的人在位执政却去陷害百姓的呢？所以，贤明的国君为百姓制定产业政策，一定要让他们上足以赡养父母，下足以抚养妻子儿女；好年成食物丰富，坏年成也不会饿死。然后督促他们走善良的道路，百姓也就很容易听从了。现在各国的国君制定百姓的产业政策，上不足以赡养父母，下不足以抚养妻子儿女；好年成里都一直忍受困苦，坏年成里则性命难保。像这样，百姓连保全性命都唯恐来不及，哪里还有什么工夫来修养礼仪呢？

Lacking a steady livelihood but having a steady original

heart – only the educated are capable of this. As for the common people, if they lack a steady livelihood, they will lack a steady original heart. If they lack a steady original heart, they will act absurdly, and stop at nothing. To punish them after they have committed crimes is equivalent to entrapping the people. How could a benevolent man rule and at the same time entrap his people? Therefore the wise and able ruler will regulate the livelihood of his people, so as to make sure they have enough to support their parents, and their wives and children. In good years they will have plenty to eat, and in bad years they will never starve. After achieving this you can urge them to do good, because in this case they will follow easily. Now, the livelihood of the people is so regulated, that the people have not enough to take care of their parents or to support their wives and children. In good years they always face hardship, and in the bad years they can't escape death. In such circumstances they only try to save themselves from death all the time, fearing that they will not make it. What leisure have they to cultivate etiquette and uprightness?

庄暴见孟子，曰：“暴见于王，王语暴以好乐，暴未有以对也。”曰：“好乐何如？”孟子曰：“王之好乐甚，则齐国其庶几乎！”

他日见于王曰："王尝语庄子以好乐，有诸？"

王变乎色，曰："寡人非能好先王之乐也，直好世俗之乐耳。"

曰："王之好乐甚，则齐其庶几乎！今之乐犹古之乐也。"

曰："可得闻与？"

曰："独乐乐，与人乐乐，孰乐？"

曰："不若与人。"

曰："与少乐乐，与众乐乐，孰乐？"

曰："不若与众。"

"臣请为王言乐：今王鼓乐于此，百姓闻王钟鼓之声，管钥之音，举疾首蹙頞而相告曰：'吾王之好鼓乐，夫何使我至于此极也？父子不相见，兄弟妻子离散。'今王田猎于此，百姓闻王车马之音，见羽旄之美，举疾首蹙頞而相告曰：'吾王之好田猎，夫何使我至于此极也？父子不相见，兄弟妻子离散。'此无他，不与民同乐也。

"今王鼓乐于此，百姓闻王钟鼓之声，管钥之音，举欣欣然有喜色而相告曰：'吾王庶几无疾病与？何以能鼓乐也？'今王田猎于此，百姓闻王车马之音，见羽旄之美，举欣欣然有喜色而相告曰：'吾王庶几无疾病与？何以能田猎也？'此无他，与民同乐也。今王与百姓同乐，则王矣。"

（《孟子》梁惠王章句下）

【译文】

庄暴来见孟子，说："我去拜见王，王对我说他喜欢音乐，我不知道怎样回答。"庄暴问："喜欢音乐怎么样？"孟子说："君王如果很喜欢音乐，那齐国就不错了！"

过了几天孟子拜见齐王，问："大王跟庄暴说喜欢音乐，有这事吗？"

齐王面有愧色，说："我不能欣赏古代帝王的礼乐，只是喜欢流行的音乐罢了。"

孟子说："如果大王很喜欢音乐，那齐国就不错了。现在的音乐和古代的音乐是一样的。"

齐王问："可以给我细讲讲吗？"

孟子说："独自欣赏音乐快乐，与别人一同欣赏音乐也快乐，哪一种更快乐？"

齐王说："与别人一同欣赏。"

孟子说："与少数人一起欣赏音乐快乐，与众多人一起欣赏音乐也快乐，哪一种更快乐？"

齐王说："与众多人一起欣赏更快乐。"

"我就跟大王谈谈欣赏音乐吧。如果大王在这儿演奏音乐，百姓听到钟鼓和箫笛笙管的声音，都觉得头疼，愁眉苦脸地相互说：'我们大王这么喜欢音乐，可怎么让我落得这么穷呢？父子见不到面，兄弟妻子分离。'如果大王在这儿打猎，百姓听到大王车马的声音，看到华丽的旗帜，都觉得头疼，愁眉苦脸地相互说：'我们大王这么喜欢狩猎，可怎么让我落得这么穷呢？父子见不到面，兄弟妻子分离。'这不是由于别的原因，是因为不让百姓和自己同样得到快乐。

"如果大王在这儿演奏音乐，百姓听到钟鼓和箫笛笙管

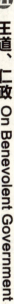

的声音，都高兴地相互说：'我们大王看来没病。否则怎么能演奏音乐呢？'如果大王在这儿打猎，百姓听到大王车马的声音，看到华丽的旗帜，都高兴地相互说：'我们大王看来没病。否则怎么能打猎呢？'这不是由于别的原因，是因为让百姓和自己同样得到快乐。如果大王让百姓和自己同样得到快乐，就能使天下归服了。"

Zhuang Bao went to see Mencius, said to him, "I had an interview with the King. His Majesty told me that he loved music, and I was not prepared with anything to reply to him." Zhuang Bao asked. "What do you pronounce about that love of music?" Mencius replied, "If the King loves music very much, the Kingdom of Qi would be quite well!"

Another day, Mencius went to see the King. Mencius said, "Your Majesty told Zhuang Bao that you love music, was it so?"

The King looked ashamed, and said, "I am unable to enjoy the music of the ancient Kings; I only love popular music."

Mencius said, "If Your Majesty love music very much, the Kingdom of Qi would be quite well! The music of the present day is just like the music of antiquity."

The King asked, "May I hear from you the proof of that?"

Mencius asked, "To enjoy music by yourself alone is pleasant, and to enjoy it with others is also pleasant, but which is the more pleasant?"

"To enjoy it with others," the King answered.

Mencius said, "To enjoy music with a few is pleasant, and to enjoy it with many is also pleasant, but which is the more pleasant?"

The King answered, "To enjoy it with many."

Mencius said, "I beg to explain what I have said about music to Your Majesty.

"Now, Your Majesty is having music here. The people hear the noise of your chime and drums, and the notes of your flutes and pipes, and they all, with aching heads and knitted eyebrows, say to one another, 'Our King likes his music as such! But why does he reduce us to this extremity of distress? Fathers and sons can't see one another. Elder brothers and younger brothers, wives and children, are separated and scattered about.' Now, Your Majesty is hunting here. The people hear the noise of your carriages and horses, and see the magnificence of your flags, and they all, with aching heads and knitted eyebrows, say to one another, 'Our King likes his hunting as such! But why does he reduce us to this extremity of distress? Fathers and sons can't see one another. Elder brothers and younger brothers, wives and children, are separated and scattered about.' Their feeling thus is from no other reason but that you do not allow the people to have pleasure as well as yourself.

"Now, Your Majesty is having music here. The people hear the noise of your chime and drums, and the notes of your flutes and pipes, and they are all delighted, and with joyful looks, say to one another, 'It seems our King were free from all sickness! If he were not, how could he enjoy this music?' Now, your Majesty is hunting here. The people hear the noise of your carriages and horses, and see the magnificence of your flags, and they are all delighted, and with joyful looks, say to one another, 'It seems our King were free from all sickness! If he were not, how could he enjoy this hunting?' Their feeling thus is from no other reason but that you cause them to have their pleasure as you have yours.

"If Your Majesty cause your people to have their pleasure as you have yours, all the people under Heaven will come to you."

齐宣王问曰："文王之囿方七十里，有诸?"

孟子对曰："于传有之。"

曰："若是其大乎?"

曰："民犹以为小也。"

曰："寡人之囿方四十里，民犹以为大，何也?"

曰："文王之囿方七十里，刍荛者往焉，雉兔者往焉，与民同之。民以为小，不亦宜乎？臣始至于境，问国之大禁，然后敢入。臣闻郊关之内有囿方四十里，杀其麋鹿者如杀人之罪。则是方四十里，为阱于国中。民以为大，不亦宜乎？”

（《孟子》梁惠王章句下）

【译文】

齐宣王问："周文王的狩猎场纵横各有七十里，是这样吗？"

孟子回答说："史籍上有这样的记载。"

齐宣王问："真有这么大吗？"

孟子说："百姓们还觉得小呢。"

齐宣王说："我的狩猎场纵横各有四十里，百姓们还觉得大，为什么？"

孟子说："周文王的狩猎场纵横各七十里，割草砍柴的去，捕野鸡和兔的也去，与百姓们共同用。百姓们觉得小，不是很自然吗？我刚到齐国边境，问清了贵国最大的禁忌后，才敢入境。我听说都城郊外有纵横各四十里的狩猎场，要是有人杀了其中的麋鹿所犯的罪和杀人一样。所以这纵横四十里的地方就如同国内的一个陷阱。百姓们觉得大，不是很自然吗？"

The King Xuan of Qi asked, "Is it true that King Wen's hunting park was twenty miles square?"

Mencius replied, "That's what the records say."

"Was it so large as that?" saied the King.

"The people still thought it small. " said Mencius.

The King said, "My park is only ten miles square, and the people still think it large. How is this?"

Mencius replied, "The park of King Wen was twenty miles square, but people could collect firewood and catch birds and rabbits in it. He shared it with the people, and was it not with reason that they thought it small? When I arrived at the border, I asked about the taboos of your state before daring to enter. I learned that there was a hunting park of ten miles square within the outskirts of the capital, and that he who killed a deer in it, was punished like killing a person. Thus this ten miles square is a trap in the center of the state. Is it not with reason that the people think it large?"

齐宣王问曰:"交邻国有道乎?"

孟子对曰:"有。惟仁者为能以大事小,是故汤事葛,文王事昆夷;惟智者为能以小事大,故大王事獯鬻,勾践事吴。以大事小者,乐天者也;以小事大者,畏天者也。乐天者保天下,畏天者保其国。诗云:'畏天之威,于时保之。'"

王曰:"大哉言矣!寡人有疾,寡人好勇。"

对曰:"王请无好小勇。夫抚剑疾视曰,'彼恶敢当我哉'!此匹夫之勇,敌一人者也。王请大之!诗云:'王赫斯怒,爰整其旅，以遏徂莒，以笃周祜，以对于天下。'此文王之勇也。文王一怒而安天下之民。书曰：'天降下民，作之君，作之师。惟曰其助上帝，宠之四方。有罪无罪，惟我在，天下曷敢有越厥志？'一人衡行于天下，武王耻之。此武王之勇也。而武王亦一怒而安天下之民。今王亦一怒而安天下之民，民惟恐王之不好勇也。"

（《孟子》梁惠王章句下）

【译文】

齐宣王问："和邻国交往有什么原则吗？"

孟子回答说："有。只有仁者才能身为大国却服务于小国，所以商汤能服务于葛伯，周文王能服务于昆夷；只有智者才能身为小国却服务于大国，所以周太王服务于獯鬻，越勾践服务于吴夫差。身为大国服务于小国的，是乐天知命的人；身为小国服务于大国的，是敬畏天命的人。乐天知命的人可以安定天下，敬畏天命的人可以保全自己的国家。《诗经》上说：'敬畏天命的威严，可以得到平安。'"

齐宣王说："这话真高明啊！不过我有个毛病，就是争强好勇。"

孟子说："那么大王就不要喜爱小勇。有一种人，只是手按着剑、瞪着眼睛说：'他怎么敢对抗我呢？'这只是小勇，只能敌住一个人。希望大王把它扩大。《诗经》上说，'我王赫然大怒，整顿军队前进，阻止侵略莒国的敌人，增强周国的威望，回应各国对周国的期望。'这便是周文王的勇，周文王一生气便使天下的百姓得到安定。《尚书》上说："天降生一般的人，也替他们降生了君主，也替他们降生了导师。这些君主和导师的唯一责任，是帮助上天来爱护百姓。有罪的人和无罪的人，都由我负责。天下有什么人敢超越他的本分？当时有一个纣王在世间横行霸道，周武王便认为这是奇耻大辱。这便是武王的勇。'周武王一生气也使天下的百姓得到安定。现在要是大王一生气便使天下的百姓得到安定，那么，百姓们就会唯恐大王不好勇。"

The King Xuan of Qi asked, saying, "Is there any basic principle to regulate one's maintenance of intercourse with neighboring states?"

Mencius replied, "There is. But it requires a benevolent ruler to be able, with a great country, to serve a small one, for instance, Tang served Ge Bo, and King Wen served the Kuen barbarians. And it requires a wise ruler to be able, with a small country, to serve a large one, as the King Tai served the Xun Yu, and Gou Jian served King Wu.

"He who with a large state serves a small one, considers it a joy to follow the mandate of Heaven. He who with a small state serves a large one, stands in awe of the mandate of Heaven. He who considers it a joy to follow the mandate of Heaven, will settle the land under Heaven. He who stands in awe of the mandate of Heaven, will protect his state.

"It is said in the Book of Poetry, 'I regard the mandate of Heaven with reverence, and will thus live in safety.'"

The King said, "A great saying! But I have an infirmity, I love valor and desire to excel over others."

"In that case, I beg Your Majesty not to love small valor. If a man brandishes his sword, looks fiercely, and says, 'How dare he withstand me?' This is the valor of a common man, who can be the opponent only of a single individual. I beg Your Majesty to greaten it.

"It is said in the Book of Poetry,

'The King blazed with great rage,

And he assembled his troops to go on an expedition,

To stop the invasion upon Ju,

To consolidate the prosperity of Zhou,

To respond to the expectations of the states.'

This was the valour of King Wen. King Wen, in one burst of his anger, gave a settled life to all the people under Heaven.

"In the Book of History it is said, 'Heaven having produced the common people, made for them rulers and mentors, with the single duty to assist Heaven in taking good care of the people. Whoever are offenders, and whoever are innocent, here am I to deal with them. How dare anyone under Heaven do e-vil?' There was one man playing the tyrant at will in the king-dom, and King Wen was ashamed of it. This was the valour of

King Wen. He also, by one display of his anger, gave a settled life to all the people under Heaven.

"Let now Your Majesty also, in one burst of anger, give a settled life to all the people under Heaven. Then the people will only afraid that Your Majesty does not love valour."

齐宣王见孟子于雪宫。王曰:"贤者亦有此乐乎?"

孟子对曰:"有。人不得,则非其上矣。不得而非其上者,非也;为民上而不与民同乐者,亦非也。乐民之乐者,民亦乐其乐;忧民之忧者,民亦忧其忧。乐以天下,忧以天下,然而不王者,未之有也。"

（《孟子》梁惠王章句下）

【译文】

齐宣王在别墅雪宫里接见孟子。齐宣王问:"贤人也会以在这样的别墅里居住游玩为乐吗?"

孟子回答说:"对。如果他们得不到这种快乐,就会埋怨他们的国君。得不到这种快乐就埋怨国君是不对的;可是作为百姓的领导人而不让百姓和自己同样得到快乐也是不对的。国君以百姓的快乐为自己的快乐,百姓也会以国君的快乐为自己的快乐。国君以百姓的忧愁为忧愁,百姓也会以国君的忧愁为忧愁。以天下人的快乐为快乐,以天下人的忧愁为忧愁,这样还不能使天下归服,是没有过的。"

The King Xuan of Qi had an interview with Mencius in the Snow palace, and said to him, "Do able and virtuous men also find pleasure in palace like this?" Mencius replied, "They do; and if they don't get such pleasure, they blame their King. Not getting such pleasure and blaming one's King is wrong. But being the leader of the people and not sharing enjoyment with the people is also wrong. When a ruler rejoices in the joy of his people, they also rejoice in his joy; when he grieves at the sorrow of his people, they also grieve at his sorrow. There has never been such a case when a ruler feels enjoyment on account of the people under Heaven, and worries on account of the people under Heaven, but the people under Heaven don't yield to him."

王曰：“王政可得闻与？”

对曰：“昔者文王之治岐也，耕者九一，仕者世禄，关市讥而不征，泽梁无禁，罪人不孥。老而无妻曰鳏。老而无夫曰寡。老而无子曰独。幼而无父曰孤。此四者，天下之穷民而无告者。文王发政施仁，必先斯四者。诗云：‘哿矣富人，哀此茕独。’”王曰：“善哉言乎！”

曰：“王如善之，则何为不行？”王曰：“寡人有疾，寡人好货。”

对曰：“昔者公刘好货。诗云：‘乃积乃仓，乃裹餱粮，于橐于囊。思戢用光。弓矢斯张，干戈戚扬，爰方启行。’故居者有积仓，行者有裹粮也，然后可以爰方启行。王如好货，与百姓同之，于王何有？"王曰："寡人有疾，寡人好色。"

对曰："昔者大王好色，爱厥妃。诗云：'古公亶甫，来朝走马，率西水浒，至于岐下。爰及姜女，聿来胥宇。'当是时也，内无怨女，外无旷夫。王如好色，与百姓同之，于王何有？"

（《孟子》梁惠王章句下）

【译文】

宣王说："可以把仁政讲给我听听吗？"

孟子回答说："从前周文王治理岐地的时候，农民为政府耕种九分之一的田地；对于做官的人的子孙进行教育，成才的就任用，不足以任用的，则给予俸禄。在道路的关卡和市场上只进行安全检查，不征税；任何人在水中打鱼都不禁止；对罪犯的处罚不牵连妻子儿女。失去妻子的老年人叫做鳏夫；失去丈夫的老年人叫做寡妇；没有儿女的老年人叫做独老；失去父亲的儿童叫做孤儿。这四种人是天下贫穷、困苦而无依靠的人。文王实行仁政，一定最先考虑到这四种人。《诗经》说：'有钱人是可以过得去了，可怜的是那些孤苦的人。'"

宣王说："这话说得真好啊！"

孟子说："太王如果认为这话好，为什么不这样做呢？"

宣王说："我有个毛病，我喜爱钱财。"

孟子说："从前公刘也喜爱钱财。《诗经》说：'丰收的粮食堆积在田地和粮仓里。他备好充足的干粮，装满各种口袋。他召集民众，去为国家争光。准备好弓箭，准备好盾牌、矛、斧和钺，他命令队伍出征。'所以说居家的人有粮食，行军的人有干粮，这样才能率领军队前进。大王如果喜爱钱财，让百姓也得到钱财，这对施行仁政有什么妨碍呢？"

宣王说："我还有个毛病，我喜爱女色。"

孟子回答说："从前周太王也喜爱女色，非常爱他的王妃。《诗经》说：'周太王亶甫，早晨骑马而来。沿着西边的河岸，一直走到岐山下。带来爱妻姜氏女，一同选址建新居。'在那时候，没有找不到丈夫的老处女，也没有找不到妻子的老光棍。大王如果喜爱女色，让百姓也得到配偶，这对施行仁政有什么妨碍呢？"

King Huan of Qi asked, "May I hear about benevolent government?"

Mencius replied, "Formerly, when King Wen governed Qi, the husbandmen cultivated for the government one - ninth of the land; the descendants of officers were educated, the able were assigned to posts, the rest were also salaried; at the passes and in the markets, strangers were inspected, but goods were not taxed. There were no prohibitions respecting the rivers and ponds; the wives and children of criminals were not involved in their guilt. There were the old and wifeless, or widowers; the old and husbandless, or widows; the old and childless, or solitaries; the young who lost both parents, or orphans. These four classes are the most needy and helpless of the people under Heaven, and King Wen, in his formulating of policies, made them the first objects of his regard, as it is said in the Book of Poetry,

'The rich may get through life;

But the needy and helpless are pitiful!'"

The King said, "Excellent words!"

Mencius said, "Since Your Majesty deems them excellent, why do you not practice them?"

The King said, "I have a weakness. I am fond of wealth."

Mencius said, "In antiquity Duke Liu was fond of wealth. It is said in the Book of Poetry,

'Bumper crops filled the fields and barns.

He prepared abundant solid food,

filling all sorts of haversacks.

He called people together to win glory for the motherland.

With bows and arrows all ready,

With shields, spears, and axes all complete,

Only then did the march begin.'

In this way those who remained at home had their full granaries, and those who went forth to war had their bags of provisions. It was not till after this that he thought he could begin his march. If Your Majesty loves wealth, give the people power to gratify the same feeling, and what difficulty will there be in your putting in practice a benevolent government?"

The King said, "I have a weakness; I am fond of women."

The reply was, "In antiquity King Tai was fond of women, and loved his queen. It is said in the Book of Poetry,

'King Tai Dan Fu came in the morning,

Galloping his horse,

Along the banks of the western waters,

To the foot of mount Qi.

Together with the daughter of Jiang,

He chose the site for their settlement.'

At that time, there were no dissatisfied women or unmarried men. If Your Majesty love women, let the people be able to gratify the same feeling, and what difficulty will there be in your putting in practice a benevolent government?"

孟子谓齐宣王曰："王之臣有托其妻子于其友，而之楚游者。比其反也，则冻馁其妻子，则如之何？"王曰："弃之。"

曰："士师不能治士，则如之何？"王曰："已之。"

曰："四境之内不治，则如之何？"王顾左右而言他。

（《孟子》梁惠王章句下）

【译文】

孟子对齐宣王说："如果大王有一个大臣把妻子儿女托付给他的朋友照顾，自己出游楚国去了。等他回来的时候，他的妻子儿女却在挨饿受冻。对待这样的朋友，应该怎么办呢？"

齐宣王说："和他绝交。"

孟子接着说："如果司法官不能管理他的下属，那应该怎么办呢？"

齐宣王说："撤他的职。"

孟子又说："如果一个国家治理得不好，那应该怎么办呢？"

齐宣王左右张望，把话题扯开。

Mencius said to the King Xuan of Qi, "Suppose that one of Your Majesty's ministers were to entrust his wife and children to the care of his friend, while he himself went into Chu to travel, and that, on his return, he should find that the friend had let his wife and children suffer from hunger and cold. How ought he to deal with such a friend?"

The King said, "He should break with him."

Mencius proceeded, "Suppose that the chief criminal judge could not regulate the officers under him, how would you deal with him?"

The King said, "Dismiss him."

Mencius said again, "If there is not good government in your state, what is to be done?"

The King, looking right and left, changed the subject.

王曰："吾何以识其不才而舍之？"

曰："国君进贤，如不得已，将使卑逾尊，疏逾戚，可不慎与？左右皆曰贤，未可也；诸大夫皆曰贤，未可也；国人皆曰贤，然后察之；见贤焉，然后用之。左右皆曰不可，勿听；诸大夫皆曰不可，勿听；国人皆曰不可，然后察之；见不可焉，然后去之。"

（《孟子》梁惠王章句下）

【译文】

齐宣王说："我怎么才能识别那些缺乏才能的人而不用他呢？"

孟子回答说："国君选拔贤德的人，在不得已的时候，要把地位低的人提拔到地位高的人之上，把关系疏远的人提拔到关系亲近的人之上，这能不慎重吗？身边的人都说某人贤德，不可轻信；各位大夫都说某人贤德，也不可轻信；全国的人都说某人贤德，也要去考察他；发现他确实贤德，再任用他。身边的人都说某人不好，不可轻信；各位大夫都说某人不好，也不可轻信；全国的人都说某人不好，就要去考查他，发现他确实不好，再罢免他。"

The King Xuan of Qi asked Mencius, "How shall I know a man is not able so that I won't appoint him?"

Mencius replied，"The ruler of a state should select virtuous and able men，and when he has no alternative he should recruit people without overstressing their origin. Since he will thereby cause the low to overstep the honorable，and distant to overstep his near relatives，ought he to do so but with caution?

"When all those about you say somebody is a man of talents and worth，you may not therefore believe it. When your senior officers all say he is a man of talents and virtue，neither may you for that believe it. When all the people in the nation say he is a man of talents and virtue，then examine into the case，and when you find that the man is such，employ him. When all those about you say somebody won't do，don't listen to them. When all your senior officers say he won't do，don't listen to them. When all the people in the nation say he won't do，then examine into the case，and when you find that the man won't do，send him away. "

齐宣王问曰："汤放桀，武王伐纣，有诸?"
孟子对曰："于传有之。"

曰：“臣弑其君，可乎？”

曰：“贼仁者谓之贼，贼义者谓之残，残贼之人谓之一夫。闻诛一夫纣矣，未闻弑君也。”

（《孟子》梁惠王章句下）

【译文】

齐宣王问：“汤放逐夏桀，周武王讨伐纣王，有这回事吗？”

孟子回答说：“史籍上有这样的记载。”

齐宣王问：“臣杀死国君，可以吗？”

孟子说：“损害仁政的人叫做贼，破坏正义的人叫做恶棍，恶棍和贼这样的人叫做独夫。我听说周武王是杀死一个叫纣的独夫，没听说是杀死国君。”

The King Xuan of Qi asked, saying, "Is it true that Tang banished Jie and King Wu took up arms against Zhou?"

Mencius replied, "That's what the records say."

The King said, "Then is it permissible for a minister to put his King to death?"

Mencius said, "He who violates the benevolence is called a robber; he who violates uprightness, is called a ruffian. The robber and ruffian we call a tyrant. I have heard of the killing of the tyrant Zhou, but I have not heard of the putting a King to death."

齐人伐燕，胜之。宣王问曰："或谓寡人勿取，或谓寡人取之。以万乘之国伐万乘之国，五旬而举之，人力不至于此。不取，必有天殃。取之，何如？"

孟子对曰："取之而燕民悦，则取之。古之人有行之者，武王是也。取之而燕民不悦，则勿取。古之人有行之者，文王是也。以万乘之国伐万乘之国，箪食壶浆以迎王师。岂有他哉？避水火也。如水益深，如火益热，亦运而已矣。"

（《孟子》梁惠王章句下）

【译文】

齐国攻打燕国，战胜了燕国。齐宣王问孟子："有人跟我说不要并吞燕国，有人跟我说要占领它。一个有万辆兵车的国家攻打一个同样有万辆兵车的国家，只用了五十天就攻打下来，这不是人的能力做得到的。不占领它，上天一定会降下灾祸。占领它，怎么样？"

孟子回答说："要是占领它会使燕国的百姓高兴，就占领它。古代的人有这样做的，周武王就是。要是占领它会使燕国的百姓不高兴，就不要占领它。古代的人有这样做的，周文王就是。齐国这样有上万辆兵车的大国去攻打燕国这样有上万辆兵车的大国，燕国的百姓却用竹筐装着饭，用壶盛着米酒来欢迎大王的军队，难道有别的原因吗？这是想摆脱他们那种水深火热的日子罢了。如果大王让他们的水更深，火更热，百姓就会转而向他人求救。"

The people of Qi attacked Yan, and conquered it.

The King Xuan of Qi asked Mencius, saying, "Some tell me not to occupy it, and some tell me to occupy it. For a state of ten thousand chariots, attacking another of ten thousand chariots, to complete the conquest of it in fifty days, is an achievement beyond mere human strength. If I do not occupy it, calamities from Heaven will surely come upon me. What do you say to my taking possession of it?"

Mencius replied, "If you occupy it and its people are happy, then occupy it. There was an ancient who acted on this principle, namely King Wu. If the people of Yan will be unhappy with your taking possession of it, then don't occupy it. There was an ancient who acted on this principle, namely King Wen.

"When a country of ten thousand chariots attacked another of ten thousand chariots, and their people brought baskets of rice and vessels of rice wine, to meet Your Majesty's troops, was there any other reason for this but that they hoped to escape out of fire and water? If you make the water more deep and the fire more scorching, they will in like manner find a way out."

齐人伐燕，取之。诸侯将谋救燕。宣王曰："诸侯多谋伐寡人者，何以待之？"

孟子对曰："臣闻七十里为政于天下者，汤是也。未闻以千里畏人者也。书曰：'汤一征，自葛始。'天下信之。'东面而征，西夷怨；南面而征，北狄怨。曰，奚为后我？'民望之，若大旱之望云霓也。归市者不止，耕者不变。诛其君而吊其民，若时雨降，民大悦。书曰：'徯我后，后来其苏。'

"今燕虐其民，王往而征之。民以为将拯己于水火之中也，箪食壶浆，以迎王师。若杀其父兄，系累其子弟，毁其宗庙，迁其重器，如之何其可也？天下固畏齐之强也。今又倍地而不行仁政，是动天下之兵也。王速出令，反其旄倪，止其重器，谋于燕众，置君而后去之，则犹可及止也。"

（《孟子》梁惠王章句下）

【译文】

齐国攻打燕国，并吞了它。一些诸侯国谋划着救燕国。齐宣王说："不少诸侯正在谋划着要来攻打我，这该怎么办呢？"

孟子回答说："我听说有凭借着七十里的国土在天下推行仁政的人，商汤就是。却没听说过有千里的国土而害怕别国的。《尚书》说：'商汤首次征伐，从葛国开始。'天下的人都信任他志在救民。他向东边进军时，西边国家的百姓就抱怨；他向南边进军时，北边国家的百姓就抱怨。都说：'为什么让我们等呢？'百姓盼望他，就像久旱盼望雨云一样。商汤的征伐不惊扰百姓，做生意的照常做生意，种地的照常种地。只是诛杀暴虐的国君来抚慰百姓，就像下了及时雨一样。百姓非常高兴。《尚书》上说：'等待我们的王，他来了我们就复活了。'现在燕国的国君虐待百姓，大王去征伐他，燕国的百姓认为这是要把他们从水深火热中拯救出来，所以用竹筐装着饭、用壶盛着米酒来欢迎大王的军队。可大王却杀死他们的父兄，抓走他们的子弟，毁坏他们的宗庙祠堂，抢走他们国家的宝器。这怎么可以呢？天下各国本来就忌恨齐国的强大，现在齐国的土地又扩大了一倍，而且还不施行仁政，会激起天下各国兴兵。大王快发出命令，放回燕国老老少少的俘虏，停止搬运燕国的宝器，和燕国的人士商议，选立一位国君，然后从燕国撤回齐国的军队，还来得及防止各国兴兵。"

Qi, having attacked Yan, took possession of it. The sovereigns of the other states planed to come to the aid of Yan.

The King Xuan of Qi said to Mencius, "The princes are planning to attack me. How should I deal with them?"

Mencius replied, "I have heard of one who with the territory of twenty miles square came to put in practice a benevolent government in the land under Heaven. That was Tang. I have never heard of a ruler with the territory of three hundred miles square standing in fear of others.

"It is said in the Book of History, 'When Tang first began his war of punishment, he started with Ge.' The people under

Heaven had faith in him. When he marched towards the east, the people in the west murmured. So did those on the north, when he marched towards the south. They all said, 'Why does he let us wait?' The people looked forward to the coming of him the way we yearn for the rain cloud during a great drought. The merchants continued their buying and selling, and the farmers carried on their farming. While he punished their ruler, he consoled the people. His progress was like the falling of timely rain, and the people were delighted. It is said again in the Book of History, 'We await our lord; his coming will be our reviving!'

"Now the ruler of Yan was tyrannizing over his people, and Your Majesty went and punished him. The people supposed that you were going to deliver them out of the water and the fire, and brought baskets of rice and vessels of rice wine, to greet Your Majesty's troops. But you have slain their fathers and elder brothers, and put their sons and younger brothers in confinement. You have destroyed the ancestral temple of the state, and are removing its precious vessels to Qi. How can such a course be deemed proper? The other states are already jealously afraid of the strength of Qi; and now, when with a doubled territory you do not put in practice a benevolent government; this will cause them to send army to oppose you. If Your Majesty will make haste to issue orders, releasing your captives, old and young, stopping the removal of the precious vessels, and saying that, after consulting with the people of Yan, you will appoint them a ruler, and then withdraw from the country; in this way you may still be able to stop the threat-ened attack."

邹与鲁鬨。穆公问曰:"吾有司死者三十三人,而民莫之死也。诛之,则不可胜诛;不诛,则疾视其长上之死而不救,如之何则可也?"

孟子对曰:"凶年饥岁,君之民老弱转乎沟壑,壮者散而之四方者,几千人矣;而君之仓廪实,府库充,有司莫以告,是上慢而残下也。曾子曰:'戒之戒之!出乎尔者,反乎尔者也。'夫民今而后得反之也。君无尤焉。君行仁政,斯民亲其上、死其长矣。"

(《孟子》梁惠王章句下)

【译文】

邹国与鲁国发生冲突。邹穆公问孟子:"我的官吏死了三十三个,百姓却没有一个为他们而死的。杀他们吧,可杀不了那么多;不杀他们吧,又恨他们眼睁睁地看着长官被杀而不去营救。到底怎么办才好呢?"

孟子回答说:"遇到天灾、人们挨饿的时候,殿下的百姓中,年老体弱的抛尸于山沟荒野,年轻力壮的到各处逃荒,这样的人差不多上千;而殿下的粮仓里堆满粮食,库房里装满财物，而官吏们不报告老百姓的情况，这是处在上位的人不关心百姓并且还残害他们。曾子说：'小心啊，小心啊！你怎样对待别人，别人也会怎样回报你。'现在就是百姓报复他们的时候了。殿下不要归罪于百姓。只要君王施行仁政，他的百姓自然就会亲近他们的上司，肯为他们的长官而死了。"

There had been an armed conflict between Zou and Lu. The Duke Mu of Zou asked Mencius, "Thirty–three of my officers were killed, but no common people died in their defence. I could sentence them to death for their conduct, but it is impossible to put so many to death. I would rather not to put them to death, but I hate them for unfeelingly watching the officers being killed and not saving them. What would be the best course for me to follow?"

Mencius answered, "When the harvest failed in calamitous years, the people suffered from hunger. The old and weak of them died in the ravines and in the wilds, and the young and strong fleed to distant places. Such people have amounted to several thousands. All the while, Your Royal Highness' granaries and treasuries were full. Your officers never reported the people's situation. This ·is a case of superiors neglecting their subordinates and inflicting suffering on them. The philosopher Zeng said, "Be cautious, be cautious. What proceeds from you, will return to you again. " This was the chance the people had to pay back the conduct of their officers to them. Your Royal Highness should not blame them. If Your Royal Highness put in practice a benevolent government，the common people will love their superiors and would die for their officers. "

滕文公问曰： "滕，小国也，间于齐楚。事齐乎？事楚乎？"

孟子对曰： "是谋非吾所能及也。无已，则有一焉：凿斯池也，筑斯城也，与民守之，效死而民弗去，则是可为也。"

（《孟子》梁惠王章句下）

【译文】

滕文公问： "滕国是一个小国，处在齐国和楚国两个大国之间。是服侍齐国呢，还是服侍楚国呢？"

孟子回答说： "这种策略不是我能想得出来的。一定要我谈，那就只有一个办法：把护城河挖深，把城墙修坚固，和百姓一起守护它。如果百姓宁可献出生命也不逃离，那就有办法了。"

The Duke Wen of Teng asked Mencius, "Teng is a small state，and lies between two powerful states，Qi and Chu. Shall I serve Qi? Or shall I serve Chu?"

Mencius replied, "The plan you proposed is beyond me. If you will have me counsel you, there is one thing I can suggest. Dig deeper your city moats; build higher your city walls; stand together with your people to guard it. If your people would rather die in its defence than flee, then the problem will be easily solved."

滕文公问曰："齐人将筑薛，吾甚恐。如之何则可？"

孟子对曰："昔者大王居邠，狄人侵之，去之岐山之下居焉。非择而取之，不得已也。苟为善，后世子孙必有王者矣。君子创业垂统，为可继也。若夫成功，则天也。君如彼何哉？强为善而已矣。"

（《孟子》梁惠王章句下）

【译文】

滕文公问："齐人准备加筑薛地的城池，我很担心。应该怎么办才好呢？"

孟子回答说："从前，太王住在邠地，狄人入侵它，他就离开定居到岐山下。不是他想要这样，是不得已。要是君主实行仁政，后代子孙一定会有成为帝王的。有道德的人开创功业，树立好的传统，为的是让后世可以继续下去。最终能不能成功，还要看命运。殿下的力量能和齐人相比吗？努力实行仁政，把其他的交给命运吧。"

The Duke Wen of Teng asked Mencius, "The people of Qi are going to fortify Xue. I worry about it very much. What is the proper course for me to take in the case?"

Mencius replied, "Formerly, when King Tai dwelt in Bin, the northern barbarians invaded it. He left it and settled at the foot of mount Qi. He did not choose to do it. He had no alternative. If a sovereign puts in practice a benevolent government, there shall be one among his descendants who will become sovereign. A virtuous man initiates the cause and lays the foundation of the heritage, so that the future generations can carry it forward. As to whether it will succeed or not, that is with fate. Can Your Royal Highness' strength match that of Qi? Do your utmost to put benevolent government into practice, and leave the rest to fate. "

以力假仁者霸，霸必有大国，以德行仁者王，王不待大。汤以七十里，文王以百里。以力服人者，非心服也，力不赡也；以德服人者，中心悦而诚服也，如七十子之服孔子也。

（《孟子》公孙丑章句上）

【译文】

使用武力而假借仁义之名的人可以称霸，称霸必须依仗国力强大。依靠道德的力量实行仁政的人可以使天下归服，使天下归服不一定依仗国力强大。商汤只有七十里的土地，周文王只有一百里的土地。用武力征服别人的，别人并不是真心服从他，只不过是因为力量不够罢了；用道德的力量使人归服的，别人会心悦诚服，就像七十个弟子归服孔子那样。

He who uses force and makes a pretence of benevolence may play the hegemonic overlord. But such an overlord must rely on solid national strength. The man who uses his virtue to practice benevolent government can make the people under Heaven yield. To make the people under Heaven yield one doesn't need solid national strength. Tang did it with a territory of only twenty miles square, and King Wen did it with only thirty miles square. When one uses his power to force people into submission, their hearts will never submit to him. They submit only because their strength is not adequate to resist. When one uses his virtue to make people submit, they are happy from the bottom of their hearts, and they submit sincerely, as was the case with the seventy disciples in their submission to Confucius.

孟子曰："仁则荣，不仁则辱。今恶辱而居不仁，是犹恶湿而居下也。

"如恶之，莫如贵德而尊士，贤者在位，能者在职。国家闲暇，及是时明其政刑。虽大国，必畏之矣。诗云：'迨天之未阴雨，彻彼桑土，绸缪牖户。今此下民，或敢侮予？'孔子曰：'为此诗者，其知道乎！能治其国家，谁敢侮之？'

"今国家闲暇，及是时般乐怠敖，是自求祸也。祸福无不自己求之者。诗云：'永言配命，自求多福。'太甲曰：'天作孽，犹可违；自作孽，不可活。'此之谓也。"

（《孟子》公孙丑章句上）

【译文】

行仁政就会有荣誉，不行仁政就会有耻辱；现在的人既厌恶耻辱却又让自己处在不仁的境地，这就像既厌恶潮湿却又住在低洼的地方一样。如果真的厌恶耻辱，最好是珍视仁德，尊敬有道德的人，使有道德的人处于一定的官位，有才能的人担任一定的职务。趁国家无内乱的时候修明政治和法律制度。这样做了即使是大国也会畏惧。《诗经》上说："趁着天晴无雨，剥些桑树根的皮，补好巢口。现在那些鸱鸮，有谁还敢欺侮我？"孔子说："写这首诗的人懂得治国的道理。能够治理好自己的国家，谁还敢欺侮他呢？"

现在国家没有内乱，趁这个时候享乐游玩，这是自己寻求祸害。祸害和幸福没有不是人自己找来的。《诗经》上说："永远要遵循天命，幸福是自己求得的。"《尚书·太甲》说："上天降下的灾害还可以逃避；自己造成的祸患可就无处可逃。"说的就是这个意思。

Practicing benevolent government brings glory, and the opposite of it brings disgrace. Nowaday people hate disgrace and yet to live in a situation that what they do is not benevolent. This is like hating moisture and yet living in a low-lying land. If a ruler really hates disgrace, the best course for him to pursue is to esteem virtue and respect virtuous people, installing the virtuous into positions of rank, giving the able jobs. When there is no internal disorder in the state, the ruler should take the opportunity to clarify the governmental procedures and legal codes. Then even states of solid national strength will be constrained to respect him. In the Book of Poetry there is the poem that goes:

"Before it's raining hard,

I has gathered the bark from the roots of the mulberry trees,

And has repaired the entrance of my nest.

Now, you owls,

Dare any of you bully me?"

Confucius said, "Didn't the writer of this poem understand the way of governing? If you are able to govern well your state, who will dare to take you lightly?"

But now the rulers take advantage of the time when there is no internal disorder in their states, and lead a life of pleasure. This is to invite misfortune for themselves. Fortune and misfortune come from no place other than yourself. The Book of Poetry says：

"Always follow the mandate of Heaven，

for happiness is in your own hands."

It is said in the Tai Jia：'It is possible to escape from the calamities sent from Heaven. But it is impossible to escape from the calamities occasioned by yourself.' These two citations reflect my point.

尊贤使能，俊杰在位，则天下之士皆悦而愿立于其朝矣。市廛而不征，法而不廛，则天下之商皆悦而愿藏于其市矣。关讥而不征，则天下之旅皆悦而愿出于其路矣。耕者助而不税，则天下之农皆悦而愿耕于其野矣。廛无夫里之布，则天下之民皆悦而愿为之氓矣。信能行此五者，则邻国之民仰之若父母矣。率其子弟，攻其父母，自生民以来，未有能济者也。如此，则无敌于天下。无敌于天下者，天吏也。然而不王者，未之有也。

（《孟子》公孙丑章句上）

【译文】

尊重有道德的人，使用有才能的人，道德、才能超出常人的人都得到任用，那么天下的士都会高兴，愿意在那个朝廷中任职。只对市场中的摊位收税，不对货物收税，或只对积压货物收税，那么天下的商人都会高兴，愿意在这些市场上设立摊位。道路的关卡只做安全检查不征税，那么天下的旅客都会高兴，愿意经过那里的道路。种地的人只需要出力耕种公田，私田不收税，那么天下的农民都会高兴，愿意在那个国家的田里耕种。居住不用交额外的税，那么天下的人都愿意做那里的百姓。真正能做到这五项的君王，邻国的百姓会像尊敬父母那样尊敬他。率领一个人的儿女，攻打他的父母，自从有人类以来，没有能成功的。像这样，就会天下无敌。天下无敌的人，是天派到人间的管理者。这样还不能使天下归服的，从来没有过。

If a ruler respects men of virtue and employs the able, so that every individual who exceeds common people in virtue or a-bility is assigned a post. Then all the scholars under Heaven will be pleased, and will want to hold a post in his court. If he only levies a rent on the boothes in the market - place but does not tax the goods, or only taxes the goods kept too long in stock. Then all the merchants under Heaven will be pleased, and will want to set up shops in your markets. If, at passes, there be an inspection of persons, but no taxes charged on goods, then all the travelers under Heaven will be pleased, and wish to make their tours on his roads. If the farmers merely have to give their aid to cultivate the government fields, and do not have to pay any additional tax, then all the farmers under

Heaven will be pleased, and will want to plough in his fields. If dwelling in his state is not subject to any tax, then all the people under Heaven will be pleased, and will want to live in his country. If a ruler is able to practice these five things, then the people in the neighboring states will look up to him as a parent. From the first birth of mankind till now, never has anyone succeeded if he led children to attack their parent. Thus, such a ruler will have no enemy under Heaven. He who has no enemy under Heaven is the minister sent by Heaven. Never has there been a ruler in such a case who couldn't make the people under Heaven yield.

　　天时不如地利，地利不如人和。三里之城，七里之郭，环而攻之而不胜。夫环而攻之，必有得天时者矣；然而不胜者，是天时不如地利也。城非不高也，池非不深也，兵革非不坚利也，米粟非不多也；委而去之，是地利不如人和也。

　　故曰：域民不以封疆之界，固国不以山溪之险，威天下不以兵革之利。得道者多助，失道者寡助。寡助之至，亲戚畔之；多助之至，天下顺之。以天下之所顺，攻亲戚之所畔；故君子有不战，战必胜矣。

　　　　　　　　　　　　　　　　　（《孟子》公孙丑章句下）

【译文】

　　天时不如地利重要，地利不如得民心重要。仅有三里长的内城和七里长的外城，敌人包围着它进攻却不能取胜。能围着城进攻，一定有合乎天时的条件；然而不能取胜，是因为天时不如地利重要。城不是不高，护城河不是不深，兵器和铠甲不是不锋利坚韧，粮食不是不多；然而弃城而跑，是因为地利不如得民心重要。

所以说，靠国家的边界限制不住百姓，靠山河的险峻保护不了国家，靠兵器的锋利和铠甲的坚韧威慑不了天下。施行仁政就能得到众多人的帮助，不施行仁政就很少能得到人的帮助。帮助的人少到极点的时候，连亲戚都背叛他；帮助的人多到极点的时候，天下的人都归服他。连天下都归服他的人攻打连亲戚都背叛他的人，会如何呢？所以有道德的人虽然不愿意打仗，但打仗就必胜。

Favorable climate is not equal to favorable geographical position, and favorable geographical position is not equal to the support of the people.

There is a city, with an inner wall of one mile long, and an outer wall of two. The enemy troops surround and attack it, but they are unable to take it. Now, to surround and attack it, there must have been favorable climate for them, and in such case their not taking it is because favorable climate is not equal to favorable geographical position.

There is a city, whose walls are very high, and whose moats are very deep, where the arms and armours of its defenders are sharp and hard, and the stores of grain are very large. Yet they are obliged to abandon the city and flee. This is because favorable geographical position is not equal to the support of the people.

So it is said: The border is unable to bound a people; the natural defence of mountains and rivers is unable to secure a state; and the sharpness of the arms and the hardness of armours is unable to terrorize the people under Heaven.

He who puts in practice a benevolent government has many to assist him. He who does the opposite finds scant support. When lacking popular support reaches its extreme point, even one's own relatives rebel against him. When being assisted by many reaches its extreme point, the people under Heaven yield to him.

When one to whom people under Heaven yield attacks one against whom his own relatives rebel, what must be the result? Therefore, the virtuous men will prefer not to fight; but if they do fight, they are ever – victorious.

滕文公问为国。

孟子曰："民事不可缓也。诗云:'昼尔于茅,宵尔索绹;亟其乘屋,其始播百谷。'民之为道也,有恒产者有恒心,无恒产者无恒心。苟无恒心,放辟邪侈,无不为已。及陷乎罪,然后从而刑之，是罔民也。焉有仁人在位，罔民而可为也？是故贤君必恭俭礼下，取于民有制。阳虎曰：'为富不仁矣，为仁不富矣。'

"夏后氏五十而贡，殷人七十而助，周人百亩而彻，其实皆什一也。彻者，彻也；助者，借也。龙子曰：'治地莫善于助，莫不善于贡。贡者校数岁之中以为常。乐岁，粒米狼戾，多取之而不为虐，则寡取之；凶年，粪其田而不足，则必取盈焉。为民父母，使民盻盻然，将终岁勤动，不得以养其父母，又称贷而益之。使老稚转乎沟壑，恶在其为民父母也？'夫世禄，滕固行之矣。诗云：'雨我公田，遂及我私。'惟助为有公田。由此观之，虽周亦助也。

"设为庠序学校以教之：庠者，养也；校者，教也；序者，射也。夏曰校，殷曰序，周曰庠，学则三代共之，皆所以明人伦也。人伦明于上，小民亲于下。有王者起，必来取法，是为王者师也。

"诗云'周虽旧邦，其命惟新'，文王之谓也。子力行之，亦以新子之国。"

使毕战问井地。

孟子曰："子之君将行仁政，选择而使子，子必勉之！夫仁政，必自经界始。经界不正，井地不均，谷禄不平。是故暴君污吏必慢其经界。经界既正，分田制禄可坐而定也。"

（《孟子》滕文公章句上）

【译文】

滕文公问孟子怎样治理国家。

　　孟子说："农业是最为急迫的。《诗经》上说：'白天去割草，晚上编成绳索。赶紧修缮房屋，来春就要忙着播种了。'百姓有一种基本情况，有稳定的产业收入才能有稳定的本心，如果没有稳定的产业收入，本心就不会稳定。本心一旦不稳定，就可能胡作非为，什么事都做得出来。等到他们犯了罪，然后才去加以处罚，这等于是陷害他们。哪里有仁慈的人在位执政却去陷害百姓的呢？所以，贤明的国君一定会谦恭待人，节俭办事，有节制地征收税赋。阳虎曾经说过："要想发财致富就不会仁爱，要想仁爱就不会发财致富。'

　　"夏代每家给予五十亩地，实行上缴五亩的收入的'贡'法；商朝每家给予七十亩地，实行助耕公田，私田不纳税的'助'法；周朝每家给予一百亩地，实行八家合作耕种私田和公田，叫做'彻'法。税率其实都是大约十分之一。'彻'是'通力'的意思。'助'是'借助'的意思。古代的贤人龙子说过：'田税最好是助法，最好不是贡法。'贡法是比较若干年的收成得一个定数。丰收年成，到处是谷物，多征收一点也不算苛暴，却并不多收。灾荒年成，每家的收成甚至还不够第二年的肥田的用费，也非收满那一定数不可。一国的君主号称百姓的父母，却使百姓心怀怨恨整年地辛苦劳动，结果是连养活父母都不够。还得靠借高利贷来凑足纳税数字。老人小孩辗转饿死在山沟。作为百姓父母的作用又在哪儿呢？可是从公田的收入中给做官的人世代俸禄，这种做法滕国已经实行了。周朝的一篇诗上说："愿雨先下到公田里，然后再落到私田里。'只有助法才有共田，所以周朝也实行助法。

"此外，还要办学校来教育百姓。'庠'是教养的意思；'校'是教育的意思；'序'是习射的意思。夏代叫'校'，商代叫'序'，周朝叫'庠'，至于大学，三代都叫'学'，都是阐明人和人之间的必然关系的。处于上层的人明白了人和人之间的必然关系，百姓间就会亲密。如果有别的国君想实行仁政，一定会仿效，这样滕国就做了诸王的老师。

"《诗经》上说：'岐周虽然是古老的国家，却承担了崭新的天命。'这是称赞文王的话。大王努力实行吧，也会让你的国家焕然一新。"

滕文公派毕战向孟子详细询问井田制。

孟子说："你的国君要实行仁政，选择你来主持井田制。你一定要好好干。实行仁政一定要从划界分田开始。田界划分不正确，井田的大小就不均匀，收田租就不会有公平的办法。所以暴虐的君王和贪官污吏就一定想取消正确的田界。田界正确了，把田地分给农民和制定官吏的俸禄，都可以容易地完成了。"

The Duke Wen of Teng asked Mencius about the proper way of administering a country.

Mencius said, "Agriculture is the most urgent. It is said in the Book of Poetry,

'In the daytime collect the grass,

And at night twist it into ropes;

Lose no time in repairing the houses,

For we must begin sowing in the coming spring. '

The way of the people is this: If they have a steady livelihood, they will have a steady original heart; if they lack a
steady livelihood, they will lack a steady original heart. If they
lack a steady original heart, they will act absurdly, and stop at
nothing. To punish them after they have committed crimes is e-
quivalent to entrapping the people. How could a benevolent
man rule and at the same time entrap his people? Therefore, a
wise and able ruler will be modest, courteous, and economical,
collecting taxes moderately. Yang Hu said, 'He who seeks to
get rich will not be benevolent. He who wishes to be benevolent
will not get rich. '

"In Xia dynasty each household was given ten acres of arable land, and each household would turn over the income of one
acre to the state. This tax system was called 'tribute'. In
Shang dynasty each household was given fifteen acres of arable
land, and each household would assist in sowing the public
land. This tax system was called 'assistance'. In Zhou dynasty
each household was given twenty acres of arable land, and eight
households would cooperate in sowing their private land and the
public land. This tax system was called 'cooperation'. In real-
ity, the tax rate in all these was similar to tithe. 'Cooperation'

means 'concerted effort.' 'Assistance' means 'drawing support from.' Long Zi, an ancient man of virtue, said, 'There is no better system than the system of assistance; we'd better not to use the system of tribute.' By the tribute system, the regular taxable amount was fixed by taking the average of several years. In years of good harvests, when the grain lies about in abundance, much might be taken without its being tyrannical, but the actual collection would be the same. But in years of bad harvests, the produce being not sufficient to repay the manuring of the fields, this system still requires the taking of the full amount. When the sovereign of a state, who is known as the parent of the people, causes the people, harboring resentment, toil all the year round; yet the produce is insufficient to nourish their parents. They have to borrow usury to pay tax. The old and young of the people suffer hunger and die in gullies. In that case, where is his parental relation to the people? But the system of hereditary salaries is already observed in Teng. It is said in a poem of Zhou dynasty, 'May the rain come down first on the public field, and then upon our private fields.' It is only in the system of assistance that there is a public field, and from this passage we know that even in the Zhou dynasty this system was also put into practice.

"In addition, a ruler should set up schools to educate the people, for example, 'Xiang', 'Xu', 'Xue', and 'Xiao'.

'Xiang' means 'breeding'. 'Xiao' means 'education'. 'Xu' means 'archery'. In Xia dynasty the name 'Xiao' was used; in Shang dynasty, that of 'Xu'; and by the Zhou dynasty, that of 'Xiang'. As to the 'Xue', they belonged to the three dynasties, and by that name. The object of them all is to clarify the inexorable relations between individuals. When the upper classes of society understand the inexorable relations between individuals, kindly feeling will prevail among the people. Should a sovereign determine to practice a benevolent government, he will certainly come and take an example from you; and thus you will be the teacher of the sage King.

"It is said in the Book of Poetry,

'Although Zhou was an old country,

It received a new mandate of Heaven.'

That is to chant the praises of King Wen. If your Royal Highness put them into practice, then your country will acquire a completely new look."

The Duke afterwards sent Bi Zhan to consult Mencius about the "nine squares" system of dividing the land.

Mencius said to him, "Since your sovereign wishes to practice a benevolent government, and has appointed you to take charge of this task, you must exert yourself to the utmost.

Now, the first thing towards a benevolent government must be to lay down the boundaries of land. If the boundaries be not defined properly, the division of the land into squares will not be equal, and the produce available for farm rent will not be fairly distributed. So, tyrannical rulers and corrupt officials are sure to create confusion in the defining of the boundaries. When the boundaries have been correctly defined, the division of the fields and the regulation of officials' salary may be determined easily afterwards. "

有大人之事，有小人之事。且一人之身，而百工之所为备。如必自为而后用之，是率天下而路也。故曰：或劳心，或劳力；劳心者治人，劳力者治于人；治于人者食人，治人者食于人：天下之通义也。

（《孟子》滕文公章句上）

【译文】

官吏有官吏的事，百姓有百姓的事。况且，每一个人所需要的生活资料都要靠各种工匠的产品才能齐备。如果都一定要自己亲手做成才能使用，那就是率领天下的人疲于奔命。所以说：有的人从事脑力劳动，有的人从事体力劳动；脑力劳动者指导别人，体力劳动者受人指导；受人指导的人上缴税赋，指导别人的人靠税赋供养：这是天下通行的原则。

Government officials have their proper business, and common people have their proper business. Besides, for any single individual, the necessaries of life can only be completed by products of various craftsmen. If one must first make them for his own use, this way of doing would keep all the people under Heaven constantly on the run. Hence, some people do mental work, and some do physical work. Mental workers guide others, and physical workers are guided by others. Those who are guided by others support them; those who guide others are supported by them. This is a principle recognized throughout the land under Heaven.

　　戴盈之曰："什一，去关市之征，今兹未能。请轻之，以待来年，然后已，何如？"

　　孟子曰："今有人日攘其邻之鸡者，或告之曰：'是非君子之道。'曰：'请损之，月攘一鸡，以待来年，然后已。'如知其非义，斯速已矣，何待来年。"

（《孟子》滕文公章句下）

【译文】

　　戴盈之说："实行井田制的十分之一税率，免除关卡和市场上的征税，今年还做不到。请让我们先减轻一些，到明年再彻底实行，怎么样？"

孟子说："有个人每天进了邻居家的院子就偷一只鸡，有人告诫他说：'这不是正派人的做法。'他说：'请让我先减少一些，每月偷一只，等到明年再彻底不偷。'如果知道这种行为不正当，就应该赶快停止，为什么要等到明年呢？"

　　Dai Ying Zhi said to Mencius, "In this year, I am not able to do with the levying of a tithe in accordance with the "nine squares" system of dividing the land, and abolish the duties charged at the passes and in the markets. Please allow me to lighten the taxes and the duties, and I will make an end of them next year. How about that?"

　　Mencius said, "Here is a man, who every day steals one of his neighbor's strayed fowls. Some one says to him, 'Such is not the way of a decent person.' And he replies, 'Please allow me to diminish my appropriations, and I will take only one fowl a month, until next year, when I will make an end of the it.' If you know that the practice is unrighteous, then you ought to make an end of it at once. Why wait till next year?"

　　孔子曰："道二：仁与不仁而已矣。"

　　　　　　　　　　　　　　（《孟子》离娄章句上）

【译文】

　　孔子说："供选择的道路只有两条，行仁德和不行仁德罢了。"

Confucius said, "There are but two paths which can be pursued, that of benevolence and its opposite."

三代之得天下也以仁，其失天下也以不仁。国之所以废兴存亡者亦然。

（《孟子》离娄章句上）

【译文】

夏商周三个朝代获得天下是因为实行仁政，失去天下是因为不实行仁政。各诸侯国的兴衰存亡也是出于同样的原因。

It was by being benevolent that the three dynasties gained the throne, and by not being benevolent that they lost it. The rise and decline, the preservation and perishing, of all states, are due to the same reason.

桀纣之失天下也，失其民也；失其民者，失其心也。得天下有道：得其民，斯得天下矣；得其民有道：得其心，斯得民矣；得其心有道：所欲与之聚之，所恶勿施尔也。

民之归仁也，犹水之就下、兽之走圹也。故为渊驱鱼者，獭也；为丛驱爵者，鹯也；为汤武驱民者，桀与纣也。今天下之君有好仁者，则诸侯皆为之驱矣。虽欲无王，不可得已。

（《孟子》离娄章句上）

【译文】

桀纣所以失掉天下，是因为失去了百姓；失去百姓，是因为失去了民心。得到天下有方法：得到了百姓的支持便得到天下了。得到百姓的支持有方法：获得了民心就得到百姓的支持了。获得民心有方法：他们所希望得到的，替他们积聚起来；他们所厌恶的，不要加在他们的头上，如此罢了。

百姓向仁政归服，就像水要向下流，兽要向旷野跑一样。所以替深池把鱼赶来的是水獭，替森林把鸟赶来的是鹰，替商汤和周武王把百姓赶来的是夏桀和商纣。现在的诸侯如果有喜好仁德的人，那其他的诸侯都会替他把百姓赶来。即使自己不想让天下归服，也做不到。

Jie and Zhou lost the throne, because they lost the people; they lost the people, because they lost their hearts. There is the way to make the people under Heaven yield. Win the support of the people, and the land under Heaven is acquired. There is the way to win the support of the people. Win their hearts, and the people are won. There is the way to win their hearts. It is simply to collect for them what they like, and not to lay on them what they dislike.

The people turn to a benevolent government as water flows downwards, and as wild beasts fly to the wilderness. Consequently, as the otter aids the deep waters, driving the fish into them, and the hawk aids the forests, driving the little birds to them, so Jie and Zhou aided Tang and Wu, driving the people to them. If among the present rulers of the states, there were one who loved benevolence, then all the other rulers would aid him, by driving the people to him. Even if he did not wish to make the people under Heaven yield, he could not avoid it.

求也为季氏宰，无能改于其德，而赋粟倍他日。孔子曰："求非我徒也，小子鸣鼓而攻之可也。"由此观之，君不行仁政而富之，皆弃于孔子者也。况于为之强战？争地以战，杀人盈野；争城以战，杀人盈城。此所谓率土地而食人肉，罪不容于死。故善战者服上刑，连诸侯者次之，辟草莱、任土地者次之。

（《孟子》离娄章句上）

【译文】

冉求做季康子的总管，不能改变他的行为，反而把田赋增加了一倍。孔子说："他不是我的学生，你们可以斥责他，大声讲述他的罪行。"从这里看来，君主不实行仁政，反而帮助他聚敛财富的人，都是被孔子所唾弃的，何况替那不仁的君主努力作战的人呢？为争夺土地而战，杀死的人遍野；为争夺城池而战，杀死的人满城；这就是带领土地来吃人肉，死都不足以赎清他们的罪恶。所以好战的人应该受最重的刑罚，联合诸侯的人应该受次一等的刑罚，让百姓为交税赋开垦荒地的人应该受再次一等的刑罚。

Ran Qiu acted as chief officer to the head of the Ji family, whose evil ways he was unable to change, while he doubled the farm rent. Confucius said, "He is no disciple of mine. You can denounce him, stating his offences loudly." From this it can be seen that when a ruler was not practicing benevolent government, those who extorted money for him were rejected by Confucius. Let alone those who fight for their sovereigns who are not benevolent! When they fight for land, the men they slaughter fill the fields. When they fight for a city, the men they slaughter fill the city. This is leading on the land to devour human. Death is not enough for such a crime. Therefore, those who are warlike should suffer the highest punishment. Next to them that should be punished, those who unite some sovereigns in leagues against others; and next to them, those who force people to open up wasteland to pay tax.

人不足与适也，政不足间也。唯大人为能格君心之非。君
仁，莫不仁；君义，莫不义；君正，莫不正。一正君而国
定矣。

（《孟子》离娄章句上）

【译文】

国君用人不当，去指责是不够的。他们行政上的失误，
去非议是不够的。只有仁德的人才能纠正国君心中的错误。
只要君主行仁，就没有谁不行仁；只要君主行义，就没有谁
不行义；君主正直，就没有谁不正直。一旦使君主端正了，
国家就安定了。

It is not enough to remonstrate with a sovereign on account
of the mal – employment of ministers, or to blame errors of government. It is only the great man who can rectify what is wrong
in the sovereign's mind. If the sovereign is benevolent, all will
be benevolent. If the sovereign is upright, all will be upright.
If the sovereign is fair – minded, all will be fair – minded. Once
rectify the ruler, the state will be tranquil.

舜生于诸冯，迁于负夏，卒于鸣条，东夷之人也。文王生
于岐周，卒于毕郢，西夷之人也。地之相去也，千有余里；世
之相后也，千有余岁。得志行乎中国，若合符节。先圣后圣，

其揆一也。

（《孟子》离娄章句下）

【译文】

舜出生在诸冯，迁居到负夏，去世于鸣条，应该算是东方人。文王出生在岐山下的周旧邑，去世于毕郢，应该算是西方人。两地相距很远，有一千多里；时间前后相距很远，有一千多年。得志的时候在中国的作为却完全一样。过去的圣人和后来的圣人，他们走的道路是一样的。

Shun was born in Zhu Feng, emigrated to Fu Xia, and died in Ming Tiao. He was a man near the wild tribes on the east. King Wen was born in Zhou by mount Qi, and died in Bi Ying. He was a man near the wild tribes on the west. The two regions were distant from one another more than three hundred miles, and the age of the one sage was posterior to that of the other more than a thousand years. But when their wishes were realized, their conduct throughout the Middle Kingdom were identical. The earlier sage and the later sage walked along the same path.

子产听郑国之政，以其乘舆济人于溱洧。

孟子曰："惠而不知为政。岁十一月徒杠成，十二月舆梁成，民未病涉也。君子平其政，行辟人可也。焉得人人而济之？故为政者，每人而悦之，日亦不足矣。"

（《孟子》离娄章句下）

【译文】

　　子产主持郑国的政事时，曾经用自己坐的车帮涉水的人渡过溱河和洧河。

　　孟子说："这是小恩小惠，并不懂什么是公平的政治。如果他九月里修成走人的小桥，十月里修成过车马的大桥，百姓们就不会为过河而发愁了。在高位的人只要把政事治理好，就是出门让行人让路都可以。他怎么能帮百姓一个个地渡河呢？如果执政的人要去讨每个人的欢心，那时间就太不够用了。"

When Zi Chan was chief minister of the State of Zheng, he would convey people across the Zhen River and Wei River in his own carriage.

Mencius said, "It was petty favours to individuals, but showed that he did not understand the practice of government. When in the ninth month of the year the foot - bridges are completed, and the carriage - bridges in the tenth month, the people would have no trouble of wading. Let a governor conduct his rule for the general good, then, when he goes out, he may cause people to be removed out of his path. How can he convey everybody across the rivers? If a governor tries to please every-body, he will find the days not sufficient for his work. "

君之视臣如手足；则臣视君如腹心；君之视臣如犬马，则臣视君如国人；君之视臣如土芥，则臣视君如寇雠。

（《孟子》离娄章句下）

【译文】

君王把臣看作自己的手足，臣就会把君王看作与手足一体的腹和心；君王把臣看作豢养的狗和马，臣就会把君王看作和过路人一样；君王把臣看作脚下的泥土草芥，臣就会把君王看作强盗和仇敌。

When the King regards his ministers as his hands and feet, his ministers will regard their King as their belly and heart; when he regards them as his dogs and horses, they will regard him as a common people; when he regards them as the ground or grass under his feet, they will regard him as a robber and an enemy.

无罪而杀士，则大夫可以去；无罪而戮民，则士可以徙。

（《孟子》离娄章句下）

【译文】

　　士没有罪而被杀掉，那么大夫可以离开国家。老百姓没有罪而被杀掉，那么士可以离开国家。

When scholars are put to death without any crime, the senior officials may leave the country. When the people are put to death without any crime, the scholars may leave the country.

　　言无实不祥。不祥之实，蔽贤者当之。

（《孟子》离娄章句下）

【译文】

　　言论不切合实际是不好的。这种不好的后果会由阻碍选用人才的人承担。

Words which are not true are harmful. Those who throw men of virtue and talents into the shade will abide the consequence.

　　禹恶旨酒而好善言。汤执中，立贤无方。文王视民如伤，望道而未之见。武王不泄迩，不忘远。周公思兼三王，以施四

事：其有不合者，仰而思之，夜以继日；幸而得之，坐以
待旦。

（《孟子》离娄章句下）

【译文】

　　禹不喜欢美酒而喜欢有价值的话。汤恪守中庸之道，选
择德才兼备的人不看出身。文王总是觉得百姓受了伤害，总
是觉得自己还不懂仁政。武王不慢待身边的人，不忘记远方
的人。周公想要学禹、汤、文王和武王，来实践上述四事：
要是古人的做法有不适合当时的情况的，就仰着头思考，白
天想不好夜里接着想；夜里想通了，就坐着等待天亮去实施。

　　Yu hated good wine, and loved good words. Tang held fast
the Doctrine of the Mean, and employed men of virtue and talents without regard to where they came from. King Wen looked
on the people as he would on a man who was wounded, and he
thought he didn't understand benevolent government. King Wu
did not slight the near, and did not forget the distant. The
Duke of Zhou desired to learn from their examples, that he
might display in his practice the four things which they did. If
he saw anything in them not suited to his time, he looked up
and thought about it, from daytime into the night, and when he
found a way to overcome the difficulty, he sat waiting for the
morning to implement it.

齐宣王问卿。孟子曰:"王何卿之问也?"

王曰:"卿不同乎?"曰:"不同。有贵戚之卿,有异姓之卿。"

王曰:"请问贵戚之卿。"曰:"君有大过则谏,反覆之而不听,则易位。"王勃然变乎色。

曰:"王勿异也。王问臣,臣不敢不以正对。"王色定,然后请问异姓之卿。

曰:"君有过则谏,反覆之而不听,则去。"

(《孟子》万章章句下)

【译文】

齐宣王问孟子公卿的事情。孟子说:"大王所问的是哪一类公卿?"

齐宣王说:"公卿难道还不一样吗?"

孟子说:"不一样。有和王室同宗族的公卿,有非王族的公卿。"

齐宣王说:"我问王族的公卿。"

孟子说:"君王如果有重大错误,他们就劝阻;如果反复劝阻还不听,他们就改立君主。"

齐宣王脸色变了。

孟子说:"大王不要奇怪。大王问我,我不敢不老实回答。"

齐宣王脸色正常了,又问非王族的公卿。

孟子说:"君王如果有错误,他们就劝阻;如果反复劝阻还不听，他们就离开。"

The King Xuan of Qi asked about the office of high ministers. Mencius said, "Which high ministers do Your Majesty mean?"

The King said, "Are there differences among them?"

Mencius said, "There are. There are the high ministers who are persons of royal lineage, and there are those who are not."

The King said, "I'd like to hear about the high ministers who are persons of royal lineage."

Mencius answered, "If the ruler have great faults, they ought to remonstrate with him, and if he do not listen to them after repeated remonstrations, they ought to dethrone him."

The King changed countenance.

Mencius said, "Let not Your Majesty be offended. You asked me, and I dare not answer but according to truth."

The King's countenance became composed, and he asked about high ministers who were not persons of royal lineage.

Mencius said, "When the ruler has faults, they ought to remonstrate with him; and if he do not listen to them after repeated remonstrations, they ought to leave the state."

鲁欲使慎子为将军。孟子曰："不教民而用之，谓之殃民。殃民者，不容于尧舜之世。一战胜齐，遂有南阳，然且不可。"

（《孟子》告子章句下）

【译文】

鲁国打算让慎子做将军。孟子说："不用礼义教育百姓就使用他们打仗，这是祸害百姓。祸害百姓的人，在尧舜的时代是不被社会容纳的。即使一战就能战胜齐国，得到南阳，这样做也是不可以的。"

The sovereign of Lu wanted to make Shen Zi the commander of his army.

Mencius said, "To take men into battle, without imparting the idea of uprightness to them, is to ruin them. A destroyer of the people would not have been tolerated in the times of Yao and Shun. Though by a single battle you could defeat Qi, and capture Nan Yang, this way of doing things is indecorous."

今之事君者曰："我能为君辟土地，充府库。"今之所谓良臣，古之所谓民贼也。君不乡道，不志于仁，而求富之，是富桀也。"我能为君约与国，战必克。"今之所谓良臣，古之所谓民贼也。君不乡道，不志于仁，而求为之强战，是辅桀也。由今之道，无变今之俗，虽与之天下，不能一朝居也。

（《孟子》告子章句下）

【译文】

　　现在侍奉君王的都说："我能为君王开垦土地，充实府库。"现在所谓的良臣，正是古代说的民贼。君王不向往道义，不立志于实行仁政，而想帮他追求财富，等于是帮夏桀致富。他们说："我能为君王与别的国家结盟，作战必定取胜。"现在所谓的良臣，正是古代说的民贼。君王不向往道义，不志立于实行仁政，而想为他作战，等于是帮夏桀获胜。沿着这条道路走下去，不改变现在的风气，就算把天下给他，也是一天也坐不稳的。

Those who nowadays wait upon their sovereigns say, "I can open up wasteland for our sovereign and fill his treasuries." The so-called "good ministers" nowadays are the same as the persons the ancient called "traitors to the people." If a sovereign doesn't yearn for the right way, and is not determined to practice a benevolent government, to seek to enrich him is to enrich a Jie. Or they will say, "I can form an alliance with other states for our sovereign, so that our battles must be successful." The so-called "good ministers" nowadays are the same as the persons the ancient called "traitors to the people." If a sovereign doesn't yearn for the right way, and is not determined to

五 王道、仁政 On Benevolent Government

practice a benevolent government, to fight for him is to try to win victory for a Jie. If a sovereign pursues the path of the present day, and not to change the general mood of political life, were to have the throne given to him, he could not retain it for a single day.

　　白圭曰：“吾欲二十而取一，何如？”

　　孟子曰：　"子之道，貉道也。万室之国，一人陶，则可乎？”

　　曰：“不可，器不足用也。”

　　曰：“夫貉，五谷不生，惟黍生之。无城郭、宫室、宗庙、祭祀之礼，无诸侯币帛饔飧，无百官有司，故二十取一而足也。今居中国，去人伦，无君子，如之何其可也？陶以寡，且不可以为国，况无君子乎？欲轻之于尧舜之道者，大貉小貉也；欲重之于尧舜之道者，大桀小桀也。”

　　　　　　　　　　　　　　　（《孟子》告子章句下）

【译文】

　　白圭说：“我想把税率定为二十分之一，怎么样？”

　　孟子说：“你的办法是北方偏远的貉国的办法。一个有一万户人的国家，只有一个人做陶器，怎么样？”

　　白圭说：“不可以，因为陶器会不够用。”

　　孟子说：“貉国五谷不能生长，只能长黍子；没有城墙、宫殿、宗庙和祭祀的礼节，没有诸侯之间送礼宴请的礼节，也没有各种官吏和衙署，所以二十分之一就够了。现在在中原国家，取消祭祀、交际的礼节，取消各种官吏，那怎么能行呢？做陶器的人太少，尚且不能使一个国家正常运转，何况没有官吏呢？想要比尧舜十分之一的税率轻的，是大大小小的貉国；想要比尧舜十分之一的税率重的，是大大小小的夏桀。"

Bai Gui said, "I want to only take a twentieth of the produce as the tax. How about that?"

Mencius said, "Your way is that of the northern tribes. In a country of ten thousand households, would it do to have only one potter?"

Bai Gui answered, "No, the potteries would not be enough to use."

Mencius said, "In their place all the five cereals are not grown; it only produces the millet. They have no fortified cities, palaces, ancestral temples, or ritual sacrifices. There is no etiquette demands presents or entertainments between their lords. There is no system of officers and offices. Therefore, one part in twenty is enough for them. But we live in the central plains. How could we banish the ritual sacrifices and the etiquette of social intercourse, or abolish officers? If a state can't do without potters, how much less can it do without gentlemen? Those who want to make the taxation lighter than tithe are to some degree barbarians. Those who wish to make the taxation heavier than tithe are to some degree Jie."

　　白圭曰："丹之治水也愈于禹。"孟子曰："子过矣。禹之治水，水之道也。是故禹以四海为壑，今吾子以邻国为壑。水逆行，谓之洚水。洚水者，洪水也，仁人之所恶也。吾子过矣。"

　　　　　　　　　　　　　　（《孟子》告子章句下）

【译文】

　　白圭说："我治理水患比大禹还强。"

　　孟子说："你说错了。大禹治理水患，是顺着水的本性疏导，所以大禹向大海排水。现在你却向邻近的国家排水。水向上游流叫做洚水，洚水就是洪水，是仁慈的人厌恶的。你说错了。"

Bai Gui said, "My regulation of rivers and watercourses is superior to that of Yu."

Mencius said, "You are wrong, sir. Yu's regulation of the waters was according to the natural tendency of water. He therefore made the sea its receptacle, while you make the neighboring states its receptacle. Water flowing out of its channels is called an overflow. Overflowing waters are flood, and what a benevolent man detests. You are wrong, sir."

　　鲁欲使乐正子为政。孟子曰："吾闻之，喜而不寐。"

　　公孙丑曰："乐正子强乎？"曰："否。"

　　"有知虑乎？"曰："否。"

　　"多闻识乎？"曰："否。"

　　"然则奚为喜而不寐？"曰："其为人也好善。"

　　"好善足乎？"曰："好善优于天下，而况鲁国乎？夫苟好善，则四海之内，皆将轻千里而来告之以善。夫苟不好善，则人将曰：'訑訑，予既已知之矣。'訑訑之声音颜色，拒人于千里之外。士止于千里之外，则谗谄面谀之人至矣。与谗谄面谀之人居，国欲治，可得乎？"

（《孟子》告子章句下）

【译文】

　　鲁国打算让乐正子治理国政。孟子说："我听到这个消息，高兴得睡不着觉。"

　　公孙丑问："乐正子能力强吗？"

　　孟子说："不是。"

　　公孙丑问："有智慧和远见吗？"

　　孟子说："不是。"

　　公孙丑问："见多识广吗？"

孟子说：“不是。”

公孙丑问：“那先生为什么高兴得睡不着觉呢？”

孟子回答说：“他为人喜欢听取善言。”

公孙丑问：“喜欢听取善言就够了吗？”

孟子说：“喜欢听取善言足以治理天下，何况治理鲁国呢？如果喜欢听取善言，那么四海之内的人会不辞千里来把善言告诉他；如果不喜欢听取善言，一个人就会模仿他的腔调说：‘嗯嗯，这我已经知道了。’自满的声音和脸色会把别人拒之千里之外。有学识的人留在千里之外，那些说陷害人的坏话和带着讨好的表情说巴结奉承的话的人就会来。和这些人在一起，想治理好国家，办得到吗？”

The sovereign of Lu intended to invite Yue Zheng Zi to run his government. Mencius said, "When I heard about it, I was so glad that I couldn't sleep."

Gong Sun Chou asked, "Is Yue Zheng Zi a man of great a-bilities?"

Mencius answered, "No."

"Is he a man of wisdom or foresight?"

"No."

"Is he experienced and knowledgeable?"

"No."

"What then made you so glad that you couldn't sleep?"

"He is a man who would like to listen to good words."

"Is the love of good words enough?"

"The love of good words is enough for the government of the land under Heaven. How much more is it so for the state of Lu! If a minister loves good words, all the people within the four seas will make light of traveling hundreds of miles in order to share their good thoughts with him. But if he doesn't love good words, then people will say, imitating his tune, "I know it. I know it." The language and looks of that complacency will keep people hundreds of miles away. When learned men stop hundreds of miles off, calumniators, flatterers, and sycophants will come to him. When a minister lives among calumniators, flatterers, and sycophants, though he may wish the state to be well governed, is it possible for him to do so?"

以佚道使民，虽劳不怨。

（《孟子》尽心章句上）

【译文】

让百姓干对他们有利的事，百姓虽然劳苦，但不怨恨。

Let the people be employed in the project that is advantageous to them, although they may be toilsome, they will not murmur.

易其田畴，薄其税敛，民可使富也。食之以时，用之以礼，财不可胜用也。民非水火不生活，昏暮叩人之门户，求水火，无弗与者，至足矣。圣人治天下，使有菽粟如水火。菽粟如水火，而民焉有不仁者乎？

（《孟子》尽心章句上）

【译文】

搞好耕种，减轻税收，可以使百姓富足。按季节享用食物，费用有节制，财物就用之不尽。百姓离开了水和火就不能生活，可是，当有人黄昏夜晚敲别人的门求水和火时，没有不给予的。因为水和火都很充足。圣人治理天下，使百姓的粮食像水和火一样充足。粮食像水和火一样充足了，百姓哪有不仁慈的呢？

Let it be seen to that their fields of grain are well cultivated, and the taxes on them are light; so the people may be made rich. Let it be seen to that the people use their resources of food seasonably, and expend their wealth economically; so their wealth will be more than can be consumed. The people can't live without water and fire, yet if you knock at a man's door in the dusk of the evening, and ask for water and fire, there is no man who will not give them, because they are abundant. A sage governs the land under Heaven so as to cause grain to be as abundant as water and fire. When grain is as abundant as water and fire, how shall the people be other than kind?

尧舜，性之也；汤武，身之也；五霸，假之也。久假而不归，恶知其非有也。

（《孟子》尽心章句上）

【译文】

尧舜行仁义是出于本性；商汤和周武王是修身以行仁义；五霸是假借仁义之名满足贪欲。借用得久了，总不归还，结果人们还以为东西真是他们的。

Yao and Shun were virtuous by nature; Tang and Wu were so by cultivating their moral character. The five overlords of the sovereigns made a pretence of benevolence in order to seek gain. Having borrowed them long and not returned them, at last people thought the things belonged to them.

春秋无义战。彼善于此，则有之矣。征者上伐下也，敌国不相征也。

（《孟子》尽心章句下）

【译文】

春秋时代没有合乎正义的战争。一个国家也许比另一个国家略好一些，这样的情况倒是有的。所谓征，是指很好的讨伐很坏的，好坏相近的国家之间是不能够相互讨伐的。

In the "Spring and Autumn Period" there were no righteous wars. One state might be a little bit better than another. But "correction" means the very good punishes the very bad by force of arms. Similar states can't correct one another.

有人曰："我善为陈，我善为战。"大罪也。国君好仁，天下无敌焉。南面而征北狄怨，东面而征西夷怨。曰："奚为后我？"武王之伐殷也，革车三百两，虎贲三千人。王曰："无畏！宁尔也，非敌百姓也。"

（《孟子》尽心章句下）

【译文】

有人说："我善于摆作战的阵势，我善于指挥作战。"其实他们是大罪犯。国君喜欢仁德，天下就会没有敌手。征讨南边，北边的人就抱怨；征讨东边，西边的人就抱怨。说："为什么让我等？"周武王讨伐殷，只有兵车三百两，勇士三千人。周武王说："不要怕！我是来安定你们的，我不是来和百姓为敌。"

There are men who say, "I am good at deploying the ranks

in battle array, I am skilful in conducting battles. " They are in fact great criminals. If the ruler of a state loves benevolence, he will have no enemy under Heaven. When Tang marched towards the south, the people in the north murmured. So did those on the west, when he marched towards the east. Their all said, "Why does he let us wait?" When King Wu punished Yin, he had only three hundred chariots, and three thousand warriors. The King Wu said, "Do not fear! I am here to restore your stable life. I am no enemy to the people. "

古之为关也，将以御暴。今之为关也，将以为暴。

（《孟子》尽心章句下）

【译文】

古代设立关口是为了抵御残暴。现在设立关口是为了实施残暴。

Anciently, the establishment of the passes was to guard against cruelty. Nowadays, it is to exercise cruelty.

不仁而得国者，有之矣；不仁而得天下，未之有也。

（《孟子》尽心章句下）

【译文】

不仁的人得到国家，这种事是有的；不仁的人长期统治天下，这种事是没有的。

There are instances of individuals without benevolence, who have got possession of a state, but there has been no instance of individuals without benevolence, who ruled the land under Heaven over a long period of time.

民为贵，社稷次之，君为轻。是故得乎丘民而为天子，得乎天子为诸侯，得乎诸侯为大夫。诸侯危社稷，则变置。牺牲既成，粢盛既洁，祭祀以时，然而旱干水溢，则变置社稷。

（《孟子》尽心章句下）

【译文】

百姓是根本的出发点，所以最重要；代表国家的土神谷神为百姓而存在，所以排在其次；国君比两者都轻。所以，得到普通百姓的欢心的人就能做天子，即使得到天子的欢心也只能做国君，得到国君的欢心只能做大夫。国君危害到国家，人们就会改立国君。奉献的祭品丰盛，盛在祭器内的祭品洁净，祭祀按时举行，但仍然遭受旱灾水灾，人们就会改立土神谷神。

The people are the most important element in a nation; the spirits of the land and grain that stand for the state are the next; the ruler is of the least importance. Therefore, he who wins the hearts of the common people becomes emperor; he who wins the heart of the emperor can only become sovereign; he who wins the heart of the sovereign can only become senior official. When a sovereign endangers the state, the people change him, and appoint another in his place. When the sacrificial offerings have been rich, the millet in its vessels spotless, and the sacrifices offered at their proper seasons, if yet there ensue drought or flood, the people change the spirits of the land and grain, and appoint others in their place.

有布缕之征，粟米之征，力役之征。君子用其一，缓其二。用其二而民有殍，用其三而父子离。

（《孟子》尽心章句下）

【译文】

可以在夏天收布的赋税，在秋天收粮食的赋税，在冬天征劳力。有道德的人在相应的季节征收其中一种，而不征另外两种。同时征用两种百姓就有饿死的，同时征用三种就连父子也不能相顾了。

There is tax by cloth that can be collected in summer; there is tax by grain that can be collected in autumn; there is tax by manpower that can be collected in winter. The virtuous ruler will just use one in its due season, deferring the other two. If the ruler use two of these in the same season, there will be starvation among the people; if the ruler use all three in the same season, then fathers and sons are separated.

诸侯之宝三：土地，人民，政事。宝珠玉者，殃必及身。

（《孟子》尽心章句下）

【译文】

诸侯有三样宝：土地、国民和政事。如果错以珍珠美玉为宝，灾祸必定落到他身上。

The precious things of a monarch are three: the land, the people, and the government affairs. If one values pearls and jade as the most precious, calamity is sure to befall him.

孟子语录

The Quotations by Mencius

君子与小人

The Perfect Gentlemen vs. the Vulgar

陈臻问曰:"前日于齐,王馈兼金一百而不受;于宋,馈七十镒而受;于薛,馈五十镒而受。前日之不受是,则今日之受非也;今日之受是,则前日之不受非也。夫子必居一于此矣。"

孟子曰:"皆是也。皆适于义也。当在宋也,予将有远行。行者必以赆,辞曰:'馈赆。'予何为不受?当在薛也,予有戒心。辞曰:'闻戒。'故为兵馈之,予何为不受?若于齐,则未有处也。无处而馈之,是货之也。焉有君子而可以货取乎?"

(《孟子》公孙丑章句下)

【译文】

陈臻问:"以前在齐国的时候,齐王送给先生质地最好的白银两千两,先生不接受;到宋国的时候,宋王送给先生一千四百两,先生接受了;在薛地,薛君送给先生一千两,先生也接受了。如果以前不接受是正确的,那后来接受就是错误的;如果后来接受是正确的,那以前不接受就是错误的。先生总有一次是做错了。"

孟子说:"都是合乎义的。在宋国的时候,我准备远行,对远行的人理应送些路费。所以宋王说:'赠送一些路费。'我为什么不接受?在薛地的时候,我听说路上有危险,想买兵器。薛君说:'听说先生要买兵器。'为买兵器赠送的钱,我为什么不接受?至于在齐国,就没有任何理由。没有理由却要送给我一些钱,这等于是用钱来收买我。有道德的人哪里有可以被收买的呢?"

Chen Qu asked Mencius, "Formerly, when you were in Qi, the King sent you a present of 30 kilograms of fine silver, and you refused to accept it. When you were in Song, the King sent you 20 kilograms of fine silver, which you accepted; and when you were in Xue, 15 kilograms were sent, which you likewise accepted. If your declining to accept the gift in the first case was right, your accepting it in the latter cases was wrong. If your accepting it in the latter cases was right, your declining to do so in the first case was wrong. There must be one case in which you did wrong."

Mencius said, "I did right in all the cases. When I was in Song, I was about to go on a long journey. Travelers must be provided with traveling expenses. The King said, 'A present against traveling expenses.' Why should I have declined it? When I was in Xue, I was apprehensive for my safety, and wanted to buy some weapons. The monarch of Xue said, 'I was told that you wanted to buy some weapons.' Why should I have declined the money for buying self-defence weapons? But when I was in Qi, I had no occasion for money. To send a man a gift when he has no occasion for it, is to bribe him. How is it possible that a virtuous man to be bought over?"

君子所以异于人者，以其存心也。君子以仁存心，以礼存心。仁者爱人，有礼者敬人。爱人者人恒爱之，敬人者人恒敬之。

有人于此，其待我以横逆，则君子必自反也：我必不仁也，必无礼也，此物奚宜至哉？其自反而仁矣，自反而有礼矣，其横逆由是也，君子必自反也：我必不忠。自反而忠矣，其横逆由是也，君子曰："此亦妄人也已矣。如此则与禽兽奚择哉？于禽兽又何难焉？"

是故，君子有终身之忧，无一朝之患也。乃若所忧则有之：舜人也，我亦人也。舜为法于天下，可传于后世，我由未免为乡人也，是则可忧也。忧之如何？如舜而已矣。

若夫君子所患则亡矣。非仁无为也，非礼无行也。如有一朝之患，则君子不患矣。

（《孟子》离娄章句下）

【译文】

有道德的人和其他人不同的地方在于他心中的愿望，他心中念念不忘的是仁，他心中念念不忘的是礼。仁德的人爱别人，礼让的人尊敬别人。爱别人的人，别人也会长久地爱他；尊敬别人的人，别人也会长久地尊敬他。

假定这里有个人，他对我蛮横无礼，有道德的人必定反躬自问：我一定不仁，一定无礼吧，不然这种态度从何而来呢？如果反躬自问自己是仁的，是有礼的，而那人仍然蛮横无礼，有道德的人必定再次反躬自问：我是不是做得还不够？如果反躬自问自己并非做得不够，而那人还是蛮横无礼，有道德的人就会说："这不过是个狂人罢了。这样的人和禽兽有什么区别呢？对禽兽又有什么可指责的呢？"

所以有道德的人有终身的忧虑，但没有一时的痛苦。比如说这样的忧虑是有的：舜是人，我也是人；舜是天下人的楷模，值得后人学习，可我却只是一个普通人。这才是值得忧虑的事。忧虑又怎么办呢？向舜学习罢了。

对于有道德的人来说，别的忧虑就没有了。不是仁爱的事不干，不合于礼的事不做。即使有一时的祸患到来，有道德的人也不会感到忧虑。

That whereby a perfect gentleman is distinguished from other men is his intention. His mind is always preoccupied with benevolence and etiquette. The benevolent men love others. The courteous men respect others. He who loves others is constantly loved by them. He who respects others is constantly respected by them.

Here is a man, who treats me in a perverse and violent manner. The virtuous man in such a case will turn inwards and examine himself: "I must have been wanting in benevolence; I must have been wanting in etiquette. Otherwise, how should this have happened to me?" If he is sure that he is benevolent, and he is polite. However, the rudeness and unreasonableness of the other are still the same. The virtuous man will again turn back and examine himself: "I must I haven't done nearly enough." If he is sure that he has done enough, but still the perversity and unreasonableness of the other are repeated. On this the virtuous man says, "This is but a madman. Since he conducts himself so, what is there to choose between him and a beast? Why should I criticize a beast?"

Therefore, the virtuous man has a lifelong anxiety and no temporary stress. For example, these cause him much anxiety: "Shun was a man, and I am also a man. But Shun became an example to all the people under Heaven, and his conduct was worthy to be learned later generations. But I am only a mediocre person." This is the proper matter that causes a man anxiety. And what to be done to it? Just to learn from Shun. A virtuous man feels no anxiety about anything else. He does nothing which is not benevolent; he does nothing which is against etiquette. If there should befall him one morning's calamity, the virtuous man does not feel anxious.

禹、稷当平世，三过其门而不入，孔子贤之。颜子当乱世，居于陋巷。一箪食，一瓢饮。人不堪其忧，颜子不改其乐，孔子贤之。

孟子曰："禹、稷、颜回同道。禹思天下有溺者，由己溺之也；稷思天下有饥者，由己饥之也，是以如是其急也。禹、稷、颜子易地则皆然。"

（《孟子》离娄章句下）

【译文】

禹、稷处在政治安定的时代，三次从自己的家门前经过都没进去，孔子称赞他们。颜回处在乱世，住在简陋的小巷里。一筐食物，一瓢水。别人都忍受不了这种穷苦，颜回却没有改变他好学的乐趣，孔子称赞他。

孟子说："禹、稷、颜回有同样的道德。禹想到天下有被水淹没的人，就像是自己被水淹没一样；稷想到天下有挨饿的人，就像是自己挨饿一样；所以他们拯救百姓才那样急迫。禹、稷、颜回如果换一下所处的环境也会有相同的表现。"

Yu and Ji, in an age when the life was stable, thrice passed their doors without entering them. Confucius praised them. Yan Hui, in an age of disorder, dwelt in a simple and crude by-lane, having his single basket of food, and his single gourd ladle of water. While others could not have endured such misery, he did not allow his joy of learning to be affected by it. Confucius praised him.

Mencius said, "Yu, Ji, and Yan Hui possessed the same virtue. When Yu thought of there were men who were drowned, it was as if he was drowned; when Ji thought of there were men who suffered from hunger, it was as if he suffered from hunger; hence, they were so earnest in saving the people from miseries. If Yu and Ji, and Yan Hui, had exchanged circumstances, each would have done what the other did."

昔者有馈生鱼于郑子产，子产使校人畜之池。校人烹之，反命曰："始舍之圉圉焉，少则洋洋焉，攸然而逝。"子产曰："得其所哉！得其所哉！"校人出，曰："孰谓子产智？予既烹而食之，曰：'得其所哉！得其所哉！'"故君子可欺以其方，难罔以非其道。

（《孟子》万章章句上）

【译文】

从前有人送条活鱼给郑国的子产，子产让管理池塘的人把它养在池塘里。管理池塘的人却把鱼煮着吃了，回去报告子产说："刚放进池塘里，它还半死不活的；一会儿就游了起来，轻快地游走，看不见了。"子产说："它去了该去的地方啦！它去了该去的地方啦！"那人从子产那里出来后说："谁说子产聪明呢？我已经把鱼煮着吃了，他还说'它去了该去的地方啦！它去了该去的地方啦！'"所以，对于有道德的人容易用合乎情理的方法欺骗他，但难以用不合道义的方法蒙蔽他。

Formerly, someone sent a present of a live fish to Zi Chan of Zheng. Zi Chan ordered his pond – keeper to keep it in the pond, but that officer cooked it and ate it, then he came back and reported to Zi Chan, "When I first let it go, it was more dead than alive. In a little while, it began swimming about in the water, and then it swam away briskly." Zi Chan observed, "It had got into its element! It had got into its element!" The pond – keeper went out and said, "Who say Zi Chan is wise? After I had cooked and eaten the fish, he said, 'It had got into its element! It had got into its element!'" Thus a virtuous man may be deceived by reasonable explanation, but it's difficult to fool him by what is contrary to uprightness.

鸡鸣而起，孳孳为善者，舜之徒也。鸡鸣而起，孳孳为利者，跖之徒也。欲知舜与跖之分，无他，利与善之间也。

（《孟子》尽心章句上）

【译文】

鸡叫便起床，勤勉地行善的人，是舜一类的人；鸡叫便起床，勤勉地求利的人，是盗跖一类的人。要想知道舜和盗跖有什么区别，没有别的，善和利的不同罢了。

He who rises at cockcrow and practices virtue tirelessly is the same kind of man as Shun. He who rises at cockcrow and pursuits gain tirelessly is the same kind of man as Zhi. If you want to know the difference between Shun and Zhi, it is simply the difference between the thought of benevolence and the thought of gain.

公孙丑曰："诗曰'不素餐兮'，君子之不耕而食，何也？"

孟子曰："君子居是国也，其君用之，则安富尊荣；其子弟从之，则孝弟忠信。'不素餐兮'，孰大于是？"

（《孟子》尽心章句上）

【译文】

公孙丑说："《诗经》上说：'无功不受禄。'可有道德的人不种庄稼也拿俸禄，这是为什么？"

孟子说："有道德的人居住在一个国家，国君用他，就会安定富足，尊贵荣耀；学生们跟随他，就会有父子之爱和兄弟之情，忠诚待人，言行一致。'无功不受禄'，有谁比他的贡献更大呢？"

Gong Sun Chou said, "It is said, in the Book of Poetry, 'He will not eat the bread of idleness.'

How is it that we see virtuous men eating without laboring?"

Mencius replied, "When a virtuous man resides in a country, if its sovereign employs his counsels, the state comes to tranquility, wealth and glory. If the young in it follow his instructions, there will be filial benevolence and fraternal affection, faithfulness, and sincerity. 'He will not eat the bread of idleness. ' Whose contribution is greater than his?"

言近而指远者，善言也；守约而施博者，善道也。君子之言也，不下带而道存焉。君子之守，修其身而天下平。人病舍其田而芸人之田，所求于人者重，而所以自任者轻。

（《孟子》尽心章句下）

【译文】

言辞浅显而意义深远的，是好的言辞；操持得少而好的影响广泛的，是好的方法。有道德的人的话，虽然说的是眼前的事，但包含了深远的道理。有道德的人操持的，是从修养自身开始，从而使天下太平。人们的毛病在于舍弃自己的田地而去给别人的田地除草，对别人的要求很高，给自己的责任却很轻。

Words which are plain, while their meaning is far - reaching, are good words. The way which is convenient to follow, while its good influence is widespread, is good way. Although the words of the perfect gentlemen are common, but the far - reaching principles are contained in them. The way which the perfect gentlemen follow is that of personal cultivation, but the land under Heaven is thereby tranquilized. The common error of people is that they neglect their own fields, and go to weed the fields of others, expecting much from others and little from themselves.

The Quotations by Mencius

富贵与贫贱

On Riches and Honor, Poverty
and Humbleness

曾子曰："晋楚之富，不可及也。彼以其富，我以吾仁；彼以其爵，我以吾义，吾何慊乎哉？"

（《孟子》公孙丑章句下）

【译文】

曾子说："晋国和楚国的财富，是我赶不上的。但是，他有他的财富，我有我的仁；他有他的爵位，我有我的义，我为什么觉得比他少了什么呢？"

The philosopher Zeng said, "The wealth of Jin and Chu can't be equaled. Although their rulers have their wealth, I have my benevolence. They have their titles of nobility, I have my uprightness. Why should I think as inferior to them?"

齐人有一妻一妾而处室者，其良人出，则必餍酒肉而后反。其妻问所与饮食者，则尽富贵也。其妻告其妾曰："良人出，则必餍酒肉而后反；问其与饮食者，尽富贵也，而未尝有显者来，吾将瞷良人之所之也。"

蚤起，施从良人之所之，遍国中无与立谈者。卒之东郭墦闲，之祭者，乞其余；不足，又顾而之他，此其为餍足之道也。

其妻归,告其妾曰:"良人者,所仰望而终身也。今若此。"与其妾讪其良人,而相泣于中庭。而良人未之知也,施施从外来,骄其妻妾。

由君子观之,则人之所以求富贵利达者,其妻妾不羞也,而不相泣者,几希矣。

(《孟子》离娄章句下)

【译文】

齐国有一个人,家中有一妻一妾。那个丈夫每次出门,必定吃得饱饱的,喝得醉醺醺的回家。他妻子问和他一起吃喝的是什么人,他说都是些有钱有地位的人。他妻子告诉他的妾说:"丈夫出门,总是酒醉肉饱地回来;问他和些什么人一起吃喝,他说都是些有钱有地位的人,可从来没见到有钱有地位的人到家里来过,我要偷偷看看他去些什么地方。"

第二天早晨起来,她悄悄跟在丈夫的后面,走遍全城,没有一个人站下来和他丈夫说话。最后他走到了东郊的墓地,走到祭扫坟墓的人跟前,讨要他们剩余的祭品;不够吃,又东张西望地到别处去乞讨——这就是他酒醉肉饱的办法。

他妻子回到家里,告诉了他的妾,说:"丈夫,是我们仰望而终身依靠的人,现在他竟然这样。"她和妾在庭院中咒骂着,哭泣着。那个丈夫还不知道,高兴地从外面回来,在他的妻和妾面前耍威风。

在有道德的人看来，人们用来谋求升官发财的方法，能够不使他们的妻妾感到羞耻而共同哭泣的，实在太少了。

A man of Qi had a wife and a concubine, and lived together with them in his house. When the husband went out, he would get himself well filled with wine and flesh. His wife asked him with whom he ate and drank. He said they were all wealthy and honorable people. The wife said to the concubine, "When our husband goes out, he is sure to come back having partaken plentifully of wine and flesh. I asked with whom he ate and drank, he said they are all wealthy and honorable people. And yet no people of distinction ever come home. I will spy out where our husband goes."

The next day, she got up early in the morning, and quietly followed wherever her husband went. Throughout the whole city, there was no one who stood and talked with him. At last, he came to the graveyard in the eastern outskirts. He begged those who were sacrificing among the tombs for what they had over. Not being satiated, he looked about and went to another party. This was the way in which he got himself satiated.

His wife returned, told this to the concubine, and said, "It was to our husband that we looked up in hopeful contemplation, on whom we fall back. And now these are his ways!" On this, along with the concubine she reviled their husband, and they wept together in the courtyard. In the meantime the husband, knowing nothing of all these, came in cheerfully, making a show of authority in front of his wife and concubine.

In the view of a perfect gentleman, there are few ways by which men win promotion and get rich which their wives would not be ashamed of and weep on account of them.

欲贵者，人之同心也。人人有贵于己者，弗思耳。人之所贵者，非良贵也。赵孟之所贵，赵孟能贱之。

（《孟子》告子章句上）

【译文】

希望尊贵，这是人们的共同愿望。其实每个人在心中都有尊贵的东西，只是没有想到罢了。别人所给予的尊贵，并不是真正的尊贵。有权势的人使你尊贵，有权势的人也同样可以使你轻贱。

To desire to be honored is the common aspiration of men. In fact all men have in their mind that which is truly honorable.

Only they do not reflect on it. The honor which others confer is not true honor. Men of great influence can honor you, but they can make you mean again.

附之以韩魏之家，如其自视欿然，则过人远矣。

（《孟子》尽心章句上）

【译文】

有晋国的韩、魏两家的巨大财富，如果不骄傲，这个人就超出一般人很多了。

If, after receiving the enormous wealth of the families of Han and Wei, a man does not become arrogant, then he far exceeds the mass of men.

孟子自范之齐，望见齐王之子。喟然叹曰："居移气，养移体，大哉居乎！夫非尽人之子与？"

孟子曰："王子宫室、车马、衣服多与人同，而王子若彼者，其居使之然也；况居天下之广居者乎？"

（《孟子》尽心章句上）

【译文】

　　孟子从范邑到齐都，远远地望见了齐王的儿子，非常感慨地说："所处的地位改变气质，就像奉养改变体质，所处的地位是多么重要啊！难道他不也是人的儿子吗？"

　　孟子说："王子的住处、车马、衣服多半与别人相同，而王子像那个样子，是他所处的地位造成的。何况住在天下最宽敞的住宅——仁——里的人呢？"

Mencius, going from Fan to capital of Qi, saw the King of Qi's son at a distance, and said with a sigh with feeling, "One's position alters the temperament, just as the nurture affects the body. Great is the influence of position! Is he after all a man's son?"

Mencius said, "The residence, the carriages and horses, and the dress of the King's son, are mostly the same as those of other men. That he looks so is occasioned by his position. How much more should a peculiar air distinguish him who dwells in the broadest house under Heaven — benevolence!"

周于利者，凶年不能杀；周于德者，邪世不能乱。

（《孟子》尽心章句下）

【译文】

　　财力富足的人，灾荒年也不至于困窘；道德高尚的人，世道混乱也不至于迷惑。

　　A bad year wouldn't leave a wealthy man in straitened circumstances. A corrupt age can't throw a virtuous man into confusion.

孟子
语录

The Quotations by Mencius

生死与天命

On Life, Death, and the
Appointment of Heaven

太誓曰："天视自我民视，天听自我民听。"

（《孟子》万章章句上）

【译文】

《太誓》上说："上天通过百姓的眼睛看，上天通过百姓的耳朵听。"

It's said in The Great Declaration, "Heaven sees through the eyes of the people; Heaven hears through the ears of the people."

尽其心者，知其性也。知其性，则知天矣。存其心，养其性，所以事天也。夭寿不贰，修身以俟之，所以立命也。

（《孟子》尽心章句上）

【译文】

充分发挥自己本心的人，能懂得人的本性。懂得了人的本性，就知道了天命。保护好自己的本心，让自己的本性得到自然发展，就是遵循了天命。不管长寿与否都无二心，培养身心等待命运，这就是完成天命。

He who has given full realization to his original heart - mind understands his true nature. Knowing his true nature, he knows the mandate of Heaven. By retaining his original heart - mind and nurturing his true nature he is serving Heaven. Whether he is going to die young or to live to an old age makes no difference to his steadfastness of purpose, he cultivates his moral character and waits for destiny, this is the way in which he establishes his Heaven - ordained being.

莫非命也，顺受其正。是故知命者，不立乎岩墙之下。尽其道而死者，正命也。桎梏死者，非正命也。

（《孟子》尽心章句上）

【译文】

一切都是天命的安排，顺应它就会有正常的命运。所以顺应天命的人不会去站在要倒的墙下。努力尽了自己的本分而死的人，所承受的是正常的命运；犯罪受刑而死的人，所承受的是非正常的命运。

There is an appointment of Heaven for everything. If a man conforms to it he will receive normal destiny. Hence, he who has the true idea of what is Heaven's appointment will not stand beneath a dangerous wall. To exert himself to meet his obligation and then die, this is normal destiny. To die in chains is abnormal destiny.

口之于味也，目之于色也，耳之于声也，鼻之于臭也，四肢之于安佚也，性也，有命焉，君子不谓性也。仁之于父子也，义之于君臣也，礼之于宾主也，智之于贤者也，圣人之于天道也，命也，有性焉，君子不谓命也。

（《孟子》尽心章句下）

【译文】

人的口喜欢品尝美味，眼睛喜欢看美丽的色彩，耳朵喜欢听悦耳的声音，鼻子喜欢闻芳香的气味，四肢喜欢安逸的姿势，这些是人的本能。但这些能否如愿还要看命运，所以有道德的人不说这些是自己的本能，要求一定得到。父子之间的仁爱，君臣之间的义，宾主之间的礼，贤者的智慧，圣人对天道的感知，虽然这些能否得到会受命运的影响，但这些是人的本性决定的，所以有道德的人不说它们决定于命运。

The mouth desires sweet tastes, the eyes desire beautiful colors, the ear desires pleasant sounds, the nose desires fragrant odors, and the four limbs desire comfort, these are instincts endowed by Heaven. But their satisfaction is dependent on fate, so the virtuous man does not say, "it is my nature;" and is determinedly to get them. The exercise of love between parents and children, the observance of uprightness between sovereign and minister, the display of etiquette between guest and host, the wisdom of the talented, and the perception of the heavenly course by the sage, although their actualization may be influenced by fate, it is dependent on whether we can fully develop the original heart – mind. Therefore, the virtuous man does not say it's decided by fate.

盆成括仕于齐。孟子曰："死矣盆成括！"盆成括见杀。门人问曰："夫子何以知其将见杀？"

曰："其为人也小有才，未闻君子之大道也，则足以杀其躯而已矣。"

（《孟子》尽心章句下）

【译文】

盆成括在齐国做官，孟子说："盆成括离死不远了！"

盆成括果然被杀，学生们问孟子说："先生怎么知道盆成括将被杀呢？"

孟子回答说："盆成括有些小聪明，但不懂有道德的人应该知道的大道理，这是足以招来杀身之祸的。"

Pen Cheng Kuo obtained an official position in Qi. Mencius said, "He is a dead man, that Pen Cheng Kuo!" Pen Cheng Kuo was indeed put to death. The disciples asked, "How did you know he would be killed, sir?"

Mencius replied, "He was a man who was intelligent in small ways, but he had not learned the major principles of the virtuous man. He was just qualified to bring death upon himself."

附录：重要的词汇和概念

Appendix：Important
Terms and Concepts

天：

支配宇宙的力量。

Heaven：

The divine ordering principle of the universe.

命：

客观规律；自然规律。

The appointment of Heaven：

Objective law；law of nature.

天道：

天所决定的必然秩序。天道借人心的作用在人心中形成
"德"。

The way (of Heaven)：

The inexorable order that is determined by Heaven. It
forms virtues in human mind with the aid of human mind.

人道：

自然规律所决定的人生正道。

The way (of man):

The correct path of human life as endowed by the law of nature.

心：

人的沟通人和天的器官。天赋予的人的本性存在于心中，天道借助心的作用在人心之中形成"德"。孟子认为心具有产生自我意识和愿望，以及进行思考的功能。

Heart – mind：

The human organ links up Heaven and man. It's the seat of the human nature endowed by Heaven. The way of Heaven forms virtues in it with the aid of it. Mencius believed it had the functions to retain self – consciousness, to generate desires, and to reflect.

德：

天道在人心中的反映。包括仁、义、礼、智等。

Virtues：

The manifestation of the way of Heaven in human mind, in the form of benevolence, uprightness, etiquette, wisdom, etc.

（人）性：

客观规律决定的人的本性。孟子认为人的本性是天赋予的，人的本性是好的；通过修身能使内心的仁德表现出来。

Human nature：

The nature of mankind as determined by objective law. Mencius believed human nature is endowed by Heaven and is inheritably good. He held that self – cultivation can enable this goodness to manifest.

仁：
对人的真诚的爱与同情。孟子认为"仁"是天赋的。

Benevolence：

Human – heartedness; the innate goodness of human nature. According to Mencius, it's one of the ethical attributes endowed by Heaven.

义：
判断行为是否正当的内心机制。孟子认为"义"是天赋的，是人的最高行为准则。

Uprightness：

The internal mechanism that is responsible for our recognition of what is proper. According to Mencius, it's one of the ethical attributes endowed by Heaven, and is the supreme standard of human actions.

礼：
指正确的行为规则。"礼"是出于对他人的尊重和关心。孟子认为"礼"是天赋的。

Etiquette：

The code of correct conduct. It's out of respect and concern for others. According to Mencius, it's one of the ethical attributes endowed by Heaven.

智：

掌握客观规律和进行正确的道德判断的能力。孟子认为"智"是天赋的。

Wisdom：

The ability to understand the objective laws and make correct moral judgment. According to Mencius, it's one of the ethical attributes endowed by Heaven.

善：

（行为）合乎仁。

Being benevolent：

(Of one's conduct) being in conformity with benevolence.

忠：

对自己和对他人尽到职责。

Faithfulness：

Being faithful to the duties to oneself and others.

恕：

利他主义。

Fellow - feeling：

Altruism.

诚：

真实无伪。对于天而言是天道的圆满体现。对于人而言是保持天赋的本性，并体现在行为中。

Genuineness：

The truthfulness of being. For Heaven, it's the perfect manifestation of its way; for man, the retaining of one's nature endowed by Heaven and acting accordingly.

信：

指身体力行仁德。

Sincerity：

Being earnest in practicing virtues.

志：

志向；内心的道德方向。

Will：

Aspiration; the moral orientation of the mind.

气：

生命活力；充斥在宇宙中的赋予生命的力量。孟子认为它是心灵和身体间的联系。

Vigor：

Energy of life; the vital, life – sustaining force that floods the universe and animates both the universe and the individual body. According to Mencius, it's the vital connection between mind and body.

中庸：

实现道及各项道德要求要符合实际情况，既不过，又无不及，恰到好处，并持之以恒。

The Doctrine of the Mean：

In realization of the true way it's necessary to give consideration to all moral characters and real situations. The ideal is to be just right, no exaggeration, and no inadequacy. It also should be followed persistently.

君子：

在内心中形成全部"德"并身体力行的人称为君子。

The perfect gentleman：

Those who are able to form all virtues in the mind and carry out them by actual efforts.

小人：

只是出于本能地爱自己，不能把爱扩展到他人的人。

The small person：

Those who restrict their affection to themselves.

仁政：

通过道德指示和教育治理国家的方法。

Benevolent government：

The way of administering a state by moral instructions and education.

霸道：

通过暴力强迫治理国家的方法。

Rule by force：

The way of administering a state by using force.

后　记

汉英对照《孔子语录》出版后几个月就再版，说明中外读者学习中国传统文化的热情很高，这激励我们加快步伐将计划中的汉英对照《孟子语录》及早面世，以使中外读者能够看到作为儒家思想核心的孔孟之道的主要内容。

儒家思想强调道德哲学，主张用"克己"的方法，达到"爱人"、"利他"的目的，使社会和谐、世界大同。这是古代历史上人类的首次自觉。它对中华民族思想和道德特征的形成起着十分重要的作用。近世人们对儒家思想的重视则是由于它对解决现实问题有所借鉴。这也正是我们编译孔孟语录的目的。

像孔子、孟子一样对中国传统文化产生过重要影响的还有老子和庄子，我们还会编译《老子》和《庄子》的汉英对照读物，希望中外读者能够喜欢。

编者　于 2005 年 12 月

（2010.11 修订）